From Arrowhead Mountain to Yulupa

The Stories Behind Sonoma Valley Place Names

From Arrowhead Mountain to Yulupa

THE STORIES BEHIND
SONOMA VALLEY
PLACE NAMES

Arthur Dawson

First Edition

Kulupi Press
Glen Ellen, California

Maps by Mike Bobbitt, GIS/GPS Project, Sonoma Ecology Center
Cover design & layout by Lisa Fortino
Cover watercolor by Ray Jacobsen
Illustrations by the author

Portions of this book previously appeared in the *Kenwood Press* and *Tales of Glen Ellen, Newsletter of the Glen Ellen Historical Society.*

Published by: Kulupi Publishing
            5026 Warm Springs Road
            Glen Ellen, CA 95442

ISBN: 0-9661867-4-5
Library of Congress Catalog Card: 97-76375
Second Printing, November 1998

for Kyrie Elizabeth Yulupa

CONTENTS

APPENDICES:

ACKNOWLEDGEMENTS

Far from being a solitary effort, this book was nourished by many people. I'm especially grateful to Mike Bobbitt, Lisa Fortino and Rebecca Lawton for cheerfully giving many hours of their time. Their knowledge and expertise made this a far better book than I could have produced on my own. The tremendous love and support of my wife Jill sustained and nurtured this project through its long gestation.

Others who shared their knowledge and enthusiasm, and helped the process along in various ways include: Diane Smith, Lin Marie DeVincent, Susan Bundschu, Sylvia Thalman, Ray Jacobsen, Maureen Hurley, Jamie & Kristi Herold, Laura Liska, Ric Shimshock & Su Kladstrup, Jabez W. Churchill, Bob Glotzbach, Milo Shepard, Pat & Win Smith, Sylvia Crawford, Gabriel Graubner, Frankie Sottile, Jack Herold, Liz Parsons, Angela Nardo-Morgan, Richard Dale, Marion Britton, Susheel Bibbs, Dallyce Sand and Margaret Wiltshire.

For creative and literary support over the years I'd like to thank Maija Elina, Kevin Beals, Stephen Altschuler, and my writers' group: Dee Jaehrling, Midge Bracco, Keith & Georgiana Hale, and Lorraine Pasini.

Finally, the Sonoma County Community Foundation and the Sonoma Valley Education Foundation deserve recognition for funding California Poets In The Schools' project *A Song of Place*, which sparked me to begin the research that ultimately spun off into this book.

FOREWORD

With contributions from at least seven languages, our local place names are the strongest legacy we have of Sonoma Valley's many-layered history. Names like *Mayacamas*, *Sonoma* and *Temelec* have probably been used here for millenia, the survivors of nearly forgotten languages spoken by the Coast Miwok and Wappo tribes. Others, like *Agua Caliente*, arrived with Mexican soldiers and missionaries in the early 19th century, recalling the days when Sonoma was *La Frontera del Norte*, Mexico's Northern Frontier. With the Bear Flag Rebellion and California's acquisition by the United States, English became Sonoma Valley's dominant language. Carriger Creek, Bennett Mountain and Schellville are a few of the many names from the American pioneer era. Each successive wave of people has left its mark on Sonoma Valley, naming and claiming it for their own.

These stories come from many sources, some more trustworthy than others. Those interested in my methods and approach can read "Deciphering the Language of the Land" in the appendix. This book covers the area of the Sonoma Creek watershed, the natural boundary of Sonoma Valley. With a few exceptions, street names are not included–covering them would have multiplied the size and scope of this book many times. For the same reason, only a few historically significant ranch and estate names are listed.

WAYS TO USE THIS BOOK:

♦ Look up a place name you're curious about. They're listed in alphabetical order.

♦ Check out the "Historical Sketches" listed in the Table of Contents for intriguing titles like "Hand to Hand Combat With a Grizzly" or "The School That Couldn't Sit Still." You'll find them inside boxes in the text.

♦ Find out where a place is by looking for coordinates in bold italics at the end of each listing: *C-5* for example. These refer to the maps at the back of the book.

♦ Discover related entries by checking out the parenthesis below each listing, which look like this: (see also Carriger Creek, Lachryma Montis & Yulupa)

♦ Those interested in specific eras or subjects will want to consult "Place Names of Special Interest" in the Appendix.

I hope this book gives you a rich window into the past, a fresh perspective on the present, and perhaps even a glimpse into the future of this unique place called Sonoma Valley. Happy Time Traveling!

Some places listed in this book are not accessible to the public.
Please respect private property.

"Sonoma es un manantial a manantiales."
Sonoma is a fountain of fountains.

Father Jose Altimira, June 1823

ADOBE CANYON is named for an adobe house that stood at the mouth of this canyon for over 100 years. Required by Mexican law to establish a residence on his property, Juan Wilson probably built the structure soon after acquiring Rancho Guilucos in 1837. Since Wilson spent most of his time at his other rancho near San Luis Obispo, the adobe may have served as a dwelling for his overseer. Later used as a stagecoach stop between Sonoma and Santa Rosa, it was still the only building in the area when William Hood purchased the property in 1851. The adobe's crumbling walls remained visible into the 1970s. *A-1*

(see also Guilicos & Hood Mountain)

AGUA CALIENTE, Spanish for "hot water," refers to the thermal springs in the area. Ignacio Pacheco, a sergeant in the Mexican Army, was granted Rancho Agua Caliente in 1836. Agua Caliente Continuation High School (now converted to the Sonoma Charter School), where teens having difficulties at the regular high school were sent, was nicknamed "Hot Water High" by its students. *B-3*

(see also Boyes Hot Springs, Hoeppner's Branch & Wukiliwa)

ANNADEL, or "Annie's Dell," as the area of the state park was known in the late 19th century, was named after Samuel Hutchinson's eldest daughter Annie. One of the main landowners in the area at that time, Hutchinson had a farm and operated a cobblestone quarry. Southern Pacific Railroad named the stop near the Hutchinson home Annadel Station in 1888. *A-1*

(see also Bennett Mountain, Ledson Marsh & Yulupa)

ARNOLD DRIVE is named for Five-Star General "Hap" Arnold, who settled in Sonoma Valley after World War II. Taught to fly by the Wright brothers, he became the very first General of the Air Force. After his death in 1950, Grand Avenue, which ran by his ranch, was renamed Arnold Drive in his honor. *B-3*

ARROWHEAD MOUNTAIN, at Sonoma Valley's southeastern corner, got its name from a large patch of bare ground shaped like an arrowhead. Still faintly visible, this landmark has filled in with trees and bushes over the last forty years. *D-4*

ARROYO GRANDE, or "Big Creek," was the Mexican name for Sonoma Creek, which formed a boundary between Rancho Agua Caliente and Rancho Petaluma. *A-2*

ARROYO SECO, meaning "Dry Creek" in Spanish, formed part of the boundary between Rancho Huichica and the Pueblo Lands of Sonoma. *C-4*
(see also Lac)

ASBURY CREEK is probably named after preacher Francis Asbury. Born in England, Asbury was sent to America in 1771 by the founder of Methodism, John Wesley, to serve as an itinerant minister. When the Revolutionary War broke out, Asbury won the loyalty of American Methodists by refusing to return to England. He did, however, remain faithful to Wesley and convinced his followers to do the same. At the end of the war, Wesley appointed Asbury "superintendent" (equivalent to bishop) of the American church. Asbury traveled widely on the expanding frontiers of the young nation, where he recruited and mentored many aspiring preachers. Asbury died in 1816.

Until the 1960s, Asbury Creek was known for its excellent steelhead fishing. The fish population began to decline about the time the creek was channeled through a culvert under Arnold Drive. *B-3*

FIDDLING, DANCING, PREACHING AND PRAYING

When California became an American possession, the Catholic church at the former Mission San Francisco de Solano was the only Christian institution in Sonoma County. The first challenge to its religious monopoly came from itinerant Protestant ministers who served their scattered flocks by preaching at a different location each Sunday. Religious festivals called "camp meetings" were also held from time to time. One participant described them as "First fiddling and dancing, then preaching and praying."

In the early 1850s, a Methodist minister asked General Vallejo for permission to hold one of these gatherings by the grist mill in present-day Glen Ellen, which used Asbury Creek for power. When Vallejo agreed, Catholic authorities threatened to excommunicate him if he allowed the assembly to take place. Given that the creek's name matches that of Francis Asbury, "the architect of American Methodism", it seems likely the meeting did happen. Whether Vallejo was ever punished by the Catholic church is unknown.

BATTERY HILL is an old name for Schocken Hill, dating to Sonoma's days as an American military post in the 1840s and 1850s. Cannon mounted on the hill were eventually transferred to San Francisco and placed on Telegraph Hill to protect the entrance to San Francisco harbor. *C-3*
(see also Schocken Hill)

BEAR CREEK, one of the upper tributaries of Sonoma Creek, probably got its name from some long-forgotten encounter with a bear. When Europeans first arrived, Sonoma Valley was prime grizzly habitat and bears weighing fifteen hundred pounds were common. George Yount reported seeing fifty to sixty grizzlies a day as he rode over his property in nearby Napa Valley in the 1830s. During the expedition to found Sonoma Mission in 1823, Father Altimira's men killed ten bears in a few hours (they were considered "offensive to humans"). Mexican and American settlers continued the slaughter, and within forty years the grizzlies were gone.

A few black bears, members of a smaller, gentler species, still roam the Mayacamas Mountains. In 1990 one was shot pilfering a vineyard in the Trinity Road area. That same year a mother and her cub were spotted sauntering along Sonoma Creek about two miles south of Sonoma Plaza. *B-1*

HAND TO HAND COMBAT WITH A GRIZZLY

One bright morning in May of 1852, Joseph Hooker, later to become a famous general in the Civil War, set off from Agua Caliente with an Indian guide to visit a remote waterfall deep in the Mayacamas. Stopping to rest in a grove of madrones, they heard a rustling in the bushes. Peeking out between the branches, Hooker saw a half-grown cinnamon cub playing in the sunshine. Ignoring his guide's warning, he grabbed his gun and shot the young grizzly. Knowing the possible consequences of such an act, the Indian left Hooker to his fate and headed down the mountain.

Hooker dropped his rifle to the ground and had started towards his prize when a huge roar stopped him in his tracks. Before he could retrieve his weapon, the enraged mother bear burst from the bushes. With no chance to retreat, Hooker drew a hunting knife from his boot and took on the bear. The two combatants struggled for a long time, the bear swiping at Hooker with her sharp claws, while he defended himself with his knife. Badly scratched and bruised, Hooker was nearly exhausted when he finally managed to sink his blade into a vital area and the huge animal rolled over dead next to her cub.

Amazingly, Hooker suffered no serious injuries from the encounter. He made the bear's skin into a saddle and preserved its feet as a memento. The bear's feet can sometimes be seen on display at Sonoma's Depot Museum.

BELTANE was the name Mary Ellen Pleasant (nicknamed Mammy Pleasant in the press) gave her Glen Ellen ranch in the late 19th century. It may mean "House of Bell", referring to Thomas Bell, her lover and business partner. Another possibility is that she was thinking of the Celtic May Day celebration called Beltane. Or it could have been a self-jest meaning "House of the Witch": Growing up in New Orleans, Pleasant received instruction in the blend of Catholicism and African religion known as Voodoo, and many people were afraid of her presumed supernatural powers. Pleasant used Beltane ranch as a weekend retreat from city life. The railway stop near the ranch was also named Beltane. *B-2*

(see also Mammy Pleasant's Cave)

BENNETT MOUNTAIN, in Annadel State Park, was named for James Bennett, an early settler of Bennett Valley, which lies between Sonoma Valley and present-day Santa Rosa. *A-2*

(see also Mountain of the Burning Bird & Yulupa)

STEALING THE COUNTY COURTHOUSE

In 1853, James Bennett ran for State Assembly on the Settlers' Party ticket against Colonel Joseph Hooker from Sonoma Valley. Many considered the election a contest between Sonoma's established residents and the newer homesteaders in other parts of the county. Though Hooker was expected to win, the vote ended in a tie and a runoff election was scheduled. Word got around that if Bennett were elected, he would introduce a bill calling for a special election to change the seat of Sonoma County. Voters in the northern and central parts of the county liked the idea of moving the county offices from the town of Sonoma to a more centralized location like Santa Rosa. With their support, Bennett won the runoff by a narrow margin. Hooker accused the Settlers' Party of importing voters and rigging the election, but Bennett was seated in the Assembly anyway and soon made good on his promise. His bill passed the state legislature, and the election for county seat was set for September, 1854.

Meanwhile, the dilapidated adobe being used as a courthouse in Sonoma was condemned by the Grand Jury as "not fit for a cattle shed." The accompanying jail was in such bad shape that prisoners sometimes escaped by knocking holes through the walls of their cells. Despite its condition, the building's owner charged the outrageous rent of $125 a month, with 30 percent interest tacked on if payment was late.

To butter up voters, Santa Rosa invited the whole county to a huge Fourth of July celebration complete with barbecued mutton and beef, speeches, music and dancing. Five hundred people attended, and when the votes were counted in September,

Santa Rosa had won the county seat. Declaring the results invalid, the City of Sonoma prepared an appeal to the legislature.

Shortly after the election, two men from Santa Rosa hitched up four mules and a wagon and rode to Sonoma under cover of darkness. Around 3 A.M. they pulled up outside the crumbling courthouse, loaded up the county records, and made their getaway. While one of the men urged the mules on with a whip, the other prodded their rear ends with the tip of his wooden leg. They arrived back in Santa Rosa at daybreak, whooping and hollering with victory. A.J. Cox, editor of Sonoma's newspaper, lamented that they hadn't taken the courthouse too, saying, "its removal would have embellished our plaza."

(see also Hooker Creek)

BIHLER SLOUGH was named for William "Dutch Bill" Bihler, a German butcher who came around the horn to California in 1848. Settling in the area, he became a large landowner and was a stockbreeder, potato farmer, and wine maker. *C-6*

(see also Tolay Creek)

BISMARCK KNOB, on the ridge between Sonoma and Napa Valleys, refers to Prince Otto von Bismarck, who served as Prussian Chancellor from 1871 to 1890 and unified the German Empire. His nickname was "The Iron Chancellor." Formerly called Mount Nebo, this peak was renamed in 1899, the year after Bismarck died. *C-2*

(see also Carneros & Mount Nebo)

BOYES HOT SPRINGS received its name from Captain Henry E. Boyes, owner and developer of the mineral hot springs. The previous owner, in a fit of rage at his wife, filled the water tank with stones, covered it with earth, and burned the bathhouse down. After Boyes bought the property, he and his wife located and cleaned out the old tank, built a huge pool, and erected the Boyes Hotel. They were the first to make a commercial success of the springs.

Boyes, formerly an officer of the Queen's Navy, has been described as "a veddy proper Englishman". His El Mirador estate was decorated with trophies from tiger hunts in India.   Around 1900, Boyes sold the resort and retired. After being destroyed by fire in 1923, the hotel reopened four years later as the Sonoma Mission Inn. *B-3*

(see also Agua Caliente, Fetters Hot Springs & Wukiliwa)

BROADWAY was originally *La Calle Grande*, Spanish for "The Big Street". It was laid out by General Vallejo to be 40 *varas*, or 110 feet wide. *C-4*

CALABAZAS CREEK appears on Mexican land grant maps from the 1840s. *Calabazas* has several meanings in Spanish, the most common being "pumpkin" or "gourd". As this area had little or no agriculture at that time, the name suggests an abundance of some wild plant. A plant known as *Calabazilla*, called "Stinking Gourd" in English (*Cucurbita foetidissima*) was formerly common in Northern California. Today it is only found south of San Francisco.

Two other possible origins of the name are: *Dar calabazas*, meaning "to jilt" (literally "to give pumpkins"), and *calabacear*, "to flunk or fail". Perhaps there was some connection with a rejected lover. Or, being on the edge of Wappo tribal territory, it was the scene of some failed campaign, perhaps the place at which Mexicans soldiers gave up chasing a raiding party of these mountain dwellers.

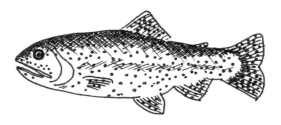

Henry Garric, who grew up in Glen Ellen, gives this description of Calabazas Creek around 1930: "There were all kinds of steelhead trout that used to come up and spawn in the creek in the wintertime. They'd back out of the deep holes into the sandy areas to spawn, and sometimes there'd be three or four pairs spawning in the sand and gravel. They are a beautiful fish and it was a lot of fun watching them. The Calabazas had other forms of aquatic life, such as eels, crayfish, turtles and suckers. This area at that time was still pretty primitive and pretty wild. People enjoyed coming up here from San Francisco because of these creeks. People would swim in Calabazas Creek in the summer, there was that much water." *B-2*

from *Childhood Memories of Glen Ellen*

(see also Nunns Canyon)

CARNEROS means "sheep" in Spanish. Rancho Rincon de Los Carneros was the name of a land grant made in this area in 1836. Bismarck Knob was once called Carnero Mountain (the word's singular form). *C-2*

CARRIGER CREEK gets its name from Nicholas Carriger, who arrived in Sonoma in 1846. Setting out from Missouri by wagon train with two sons, his pregnant wife Mary, and several other relatives, Carriger and his party spent six months making the 2200-mile journey to California. Along the way, a buffalo stampede destroyed two of their prairie schooners, several horses were stolen by Shoshones, and Nicholas' father and mother-in-law died from fever and "sheer exhaustion." On the day his father died, Mary gave birth to a daughter.

Arriving in Sonoma a few months after the Bear Flag Rebellion, Carriger joined the U..S. Navy and saw action against Mexican forces at Benicia and Monterey. He also served for awhile as a Naval Mail Carrier, traveling between Sonoma and San Rafael on horseback. During the gold rush, Carriger struck it rich on the American River. Back in Sonoma, he bought 1000 acres on the west side of the valley from General Vallejo for four dollars an acre. His ranch eventually included a large two-story house, dairy barns, fruit and nut orchards, wheat fields, herds of stock roaming the hills, and a three-story stone winery. A civic-minded man, Carriger was instrumental in getting Sonoma Valley's public school system started in the late 1850s. Carriger passed away in 1885 at the age of 70, his wife Mary following him a few years later.

It was along Carriger Creek that a peace treaty was signed between General Vallejo and Chief Succara of the Satiyomi tribe in the 1830s. As part of the agreement, Vallejo promised to deliver eight steers and two cows to Succara each week, while every full moon Succara was to provide Vallejo with two grizzly bears large enough to fight bulls. (Bear and bull fights were a popular form of entertainment in Mexican California.)

A few members of the Miwok tribe, the original inhabitants of Sonoma Valley, who had survived the smallpox epidemic of 1838, were living near Yulupa Springs when Carriger bought his ranch. Carriger befriended them and gave them the right to fish, collect wood, till the earth, and use the water as long as they "behaved themselves." Descendants of these people were still living on the property in the 1920s. *B-4*
(see also Lewis Creek & Yulupa)

CHAMPLIN CREEK runs through land occupied by the Champlin family for several generations. Traveling from Illinois by wagon train, Charles and Sarah Champlin first settled in Solano County in 1854. Finding that location too windy, they headed west again, finding a calmer spot on the west side of Sonoma Valley, where they bought a 274-acre ranch from General Vallejo for four dollars an acre. Charles was one of only nine people in the valley to vote for Abraham Lincoln in the presidential election of 1860. *B-5*

CHINA SLOUGH is named for a Chinese settlement that existed along its banks in the late 19th and early 20th centuries. *C-5*
(see also Chinatown, Poppe's Landing & Wingo)

CHINATOWN: Visiting Sonoma in the 19th century, you would have seen, "Across from the plaza, laundries and markets and lotteries lively with sing-song voices and pungent incense smells. One could find round coins with square holes, and men with poles across their shoulders carrying two balanced weights. One could see Chinese worshipping at shrines, holding joss sticks in front of their gods."
Not on map

from *Secrets of El Verano*
(see also China Slough, Poppe's Landing & Wingo)

CHIUCUYEM is a Miwok name associated with either the copious springs on General Vallejo's estate, the hill behind them, or both. Vallejo translated it as 'Weeping Mountain' and used the latin version of this name, *Lachryma Montis*, for his estate.

Isabel Kelly, an anthropologist who interviewed Miwok elders in Tomales and Bodega in the 1930s, thought the name might be a compound of *tcok* and *oyen*, meaning "old man creek" or "coyote creek" (*Chiucuyem* has also been spelled *Tcho-ko-yem*). *Oye* is both the name for Coyote, the trickster figure who helps create the world, and the word for old man. The form *oyen* sometimes refers to the common coyote rather than the mythological being. *C-3*
(see also Lachryma Montis & Oona-pa'is)

COOPER'S BRIDGE, originally built in 1853, was for many years the only bridge over Sonoma Creek. James Cooper, a Scotsman, ran the Blue Wing with his partner Tom Spriggs, a ship's carpenter from England. Cooper got rich off the American troops stationed in Sonoma at the time, as well as by satisfying miners' demands for gambling and alcohol. Whiskey was sold for pinches of gold dust. In 1851 Cooper purchased property south of Sonoma, where he built a house and the first bridge over Sonoma Creek. Cooper has been described as a "big, hot-tempered redhead". In 1856 he threatened to "whip" a teacher who had struck one of his sons in school. The badly frightened schoolmaster grabbed a knife and stabbed Cooper dead. *C-4*

COWAN MEADOW, high on Sonoma Mountain, was homesteaded by the Scotch-Irish Cowan family around 1850. Though they later abandoned the property (probably during the depression of the 1880s), members of the family remained in the area. Jim Cowan, second cousin to the original Cowans, hauled rock and other materials for the Wolf House. His son Hazen was Jack London's foreman. Described as big, hardheaded Irishmen, Hazen and his brother Norman were champion rodeo riders.

Milo Shephard, Jack London's great-nephew, remembers Norman as "a real tough cowboy type. One time when he was on the rodeo circuit in the '20s, he broke his leg and needed to win the saddle bronc competition to win the World's Champion All Around Cowboy in Salinas, to get enough points. He sat all night in an icehouse with his leg between two blocks of ice and went out and rode the next day and won the contest." *A-3*

(see also Jack London State Park)

from *Childhood Memories of Glen Ellen*

DIAMOND A was never a cattle brand. "A" is for the Anderson family, owners of the Bank of California, who created the name when they subdivided the land for this low-density residential area on Sonoma Mountain. *A-3*

DEER CAMP, on Sonoma Mountain, was established after World War I as a hunters' retreat. Marlin Sassenrath remembers "We typically stayed at Deer Camp all weekend and usually got several deer, which were divided among the members." He says the younger members "did most of the 'dogging,' flushed the deer out, and the older gentlemen usually sat on what we called the 'stand.' The deer ran by them and became a target for them." *A-3*

from *Childhood Memories of Glen Ellen*

DOWDALL CREEK was named after the Dowdall family, Irish immigrants who settled on land north of Nicholas Carriger's place in the 19th century. One stormy night, Mrs. Dowdall was in labor when the house began sliding downhill. Luckily the house stopped when it hit the mud at the bottom, and her son Nick arrived with no further complications. *B-3*

ELDRIDGE was named for ship's captain Oliver Eldridge. In the process of moving the state hospital from Santa Clara to Sonoma in 1890, State Senator Murphy chose Eldridge and a Mr. Gibbs to select a suitable site. They chose a 1600-acre property just south of Glen Ellen, which the state purchased for $51,000. Originally called "The California Home for the Care and Training of Feeble-minded Children," the institution went through several name changes before becoming "The Sonoma Developmental Center" in 1988.

An island town surrounded by Glen Ellen, at one time Eldridge was the larger community, with a population of 4,500 and its own railway station. Eldridge still has its own postmaster and zip code. *B-3*

EL VERANO means "summer" in Spanish. Developer George Maxwell said he chose the name because "the climate here is considered about perfect." After the Santa Rosa & Carquinez Railroad arrived in the valley, the townsite was laid out near the tracks. Lots sold for $80, while twenty-acre parcels fetched up to $550. During the spring of 1888, the railroad gave free excursions to over 500 people for the purpose of auctioning lots. Some bidders got a free house with their land. For a couple of years the new community boomed and even had its own newspaper called *The Whistler* (after the steam engine's whistle). Things went bust when Maxwell was unable to guarantee property titles. The newspaper closed down, the project was labeled a "scam," and Maxwell moved his family to San Jose. *B-3 & B-4*
(see also Maxwell Park)

Built in 1874, the sternwheel steamer Sonoma *provided freight and passenger service between Embarcadero and San Francisco.*

EMBARCADERO, meaning "pier" or "landing place" in Spanish, was at the upper limit of navigation on Sonoma Creek. The site was used for landing small craft as early as 1823. Scheduled passenger and freight service began around 1850 and continued to the end of the 19th century. The following description, adapted from *Saga of Sonoma*, shows what a busy place Embarcadero was in those days:

"Sonoma Creek was the only outlet for shipping and a large volume of business gave much prominence to Embarcadero. Teams of four and six horses, or two and three yoke of oxen, hauled wine, wood, etc. from valley points as far north as Los Guilicos [Kenwood]. Cargoes of farm products furnished outgoing shipments, while lumber and general merchandise made up return loads. Many large buildings lined the banks of the creek wherein hay, grain, and other valley products were stored awaiting sale and shipment to the markets. A very large business was done in firewood; many hundreds of cords were stacked to be shipped to San Francisco and Vallejo, the latter especially being an excellent market for this product."

Over time, as the channel filled with silt, the use of sloops gave way to boats of lesser draught and even flat-bottomed scows. Erosion upstream was responsible for this, much of it probably from the denuded hillsides left by cutting the very firewood that was being shipped out from the Embarcadero. *C-5*

(see also McGill's Landing, Norfolk, Poppe's Landing, San Luis, Schellville, Stofen's Landing & Wingo)

FETTERS HOT SPRINGS got its name from George Fetters. Originally from Pittsburgh, Pennsylvania, Fetters bought property in Sonoma Valley in 1907. Drilling for mineral water, he struck an underground hot spring. *B-3*

(see also Agua Caliente, Boyes Hot Springs & Wukiliwa)

FIRST STREET EAST was called *Cuartel* in Mexican days, because it ran to the *cuartel,* the soldiers' barracks.

FIRST STREET WEST was originally *Calle Huerta,* or "Orchard Street," because it passed by the orchard of General Vallejo's brother, Salvador. It was also sometimes called "Salvador Street."

FOWLER CREEK: A number of Fowlers settled Sonoma Valley in the mid-19th century; exactly which one the creek is named after is unclear. Two Fowlers worked as carpenters on Vallejo's Casa Grande while California was under Mexican rule. George Fowler was one of the first two casualties of the Bear Flag Rebellion: On an errand to procure powder for the Bear Flag Army, he and a man named Cowie were captured by a band of young Mexicans that included Bernardino Garcia, also known as "Three-Fingered Jack," and General Vallejo's brother-in-law, Jose Ramon Carrillo. Years later, Carrillo said that Garcia waited until he had the men to himself and killed them with a knife because he feared his comrades were planning to set them free. *C-5*

(see also Sears Point & Secret Pasture)

FREY CANYON was named for the Frey family, who settled nearby in 1909 and put in an orchard a year later. In 1918 newlyweds John Frey and his wife Emma bought a horse-powered haypress from the owner of Hood Ranch:

"With the help of ten strong men and twelve or more horses, they traveled over the county baling hay. Mrs. Frey remembers the horse-drawn cook wagon in which she cooked the meals for the men as they moved from job to job." *A-1*

from *Kenwood Yesterday and Today*

GLEN ELLEN started out as the name of Colonel Charles Stuart's ranch. Settling here in 1859, he named the property Glen Ellen Vineyards after his beloved wife, Mary Ellen (Glen comes from the Gaelic word *glenn*, meaning "secluded mountain valley"). As a town began sprouting up nearby, some residents wanted to call it Lebanon, but the Postal Service said the nation already had too many Lebanons and Glen Ellen won out. Stuart ended up changing the name of his ranch to Glen Oaks, which it is still called today.

After her husband's death, Ellen successfully took over management of his winemaking business, more than doubling the operation's output in one year. At a time when women could not vote and very rarely ran businesses, she was one of three "lady winemakers" in the area in the 1880s. The others were Kate Warfield, widow of Dr. Warfield, across the road in Glen Ellen and Mrs. Hood at Guilicos. *B-2*

(see also Hood Mountain, Mount Pisgah, Stuart Creek & Warfield)

GRAHAM CREEK was probably named for an early settler. The name appears in the 1877 *Sonoma County Atlas* and is mentioned in records dating back to 1853 as the source of wood for Cooper's Bridge. *A-2*

(see also Wildwater)

GUILICOS was the Spanish name for a Wappo tribe living in the Kenwood area and was also attached to their permanent village near the headwaters of Sonoma Creek. Father Juan Amoros of Mission San Rafael mentions this group in 1823 as "*la nacion Guiluc*" or "the Guiluc nation." Adding *-os* in Spanish signifies citizenship, e.g. *Americanos*, so members of the *Guiluc* tribe were *Guilucos*.

Taking into account that "*gu*" at the beginning of Spanish words often sounds like an English "*w*", the closest word in available Wappo dictionaries is *wo'lico*, meaning mush stirrer (basically a cooking spoon). Since the Mexicans were better acquainted with the Miwoks than the Wappos, *Guiluc* may be a Miwok word. Similar-sounding words in the Lake Miwok language include:

Wilik, meaning "to get, hold, catch, pick up, or pick out." Sometimes it is used to talk about how a song comes to a person, as a musician or poet might speak of getting a visit from the muse, or say "it just came to me."

Wiilok means "ashes or dust." *Wiilokjomi*, or "Dusty Place," was a Lake Miwok village near Mount St. Helena.

Scottish sea captain John Wilson was awarded the 19,000-acre Rancho Guilucos land grant by the Mexican government in 1837. (Though larger in scale, Mexican land grants were similar to homesteading in the U.S., which granted federal land to settlers.) Wilson had been sailing into Bodega Bay with cargo destined for Sonoma and picking up hides at the ranchos. When he married Ramona Carrillo, General Vallejo's sister-in-law, he changed his name to Juan to obtain Mexican citizenship papers so he could legally receive the grant. A surveyor's map added "Los" and changed the spelling to Guilicos in 1859. *B-2*
(see also Adobe Canyon)

GUNSIGHT ROCK, high on Hood Mountain, is a visual metaphor from pioneer days, its twin rocks reminiscent of the sights on a hunter's rifle. *A-1*
(see also Hood Mountain)

THE FATHER OF CALIFORNIA'S WINE INDUSTRY

HARASZTHY CREEK is named for Agostin Haraszthy, a Hungarian nobleman and army officer who was banished from his homeland for taking part in an attempted revolution. After settling in Wisconsin and Illinois, he made a trip to California searching for the perfect spot to plant experimental vineyards. Hearing of "Lachryma Montis," an extraordinary wine made by General Vallejo, he came to Sonoma Valley. Impressed by the climate, Haraszthy acquired land east of Sonoma and in the 1850s, developed the vineyards and winery at Buena Vista.

Funded by the State of California, Haraszthy traveled back to Europe in 1862 to study winemaking techniques. He returned with 100,000 cuttings of 300 varieties of grapes. Once these were propagated, cuttings from Haraszthy's vines were planted all over the state. The book he wrote, *Grape Culture, Wines and Winemaking*, became the winemakers' bible of that era. Haraszthy also produced a Zinfandel that was the first world-famous wine to come from California. In June 1862, two of Haraszthy's sons married two of General Vallejo's daughters in a double wedding at Lachryma Montis.

A double stroke of bad luck ended Haraszthy's winemaking enterprise: After ravaging European grapes, the root disease *phylloxera* reached California, devastating Sonoma's wine industry. Soon after that disaster, an earthquake brought down a section of the Buena Vista winery; 30,000 bottles of finished champagne are said to be buried in a collapsed storage tunnel.

Haraszthy himself disappeared in Nicaragua in 1869 while crossing a river on a tree trunk. Stepping on a weak branch, he fell into the water. No body was ever found and it was assumed he was devoured by alligators. *C-4*

SPIES IN THE BARN

HAYFIELDS, a grassy spur on Sonoma Mountain, was once farmed for hay. During World War II, the hay barn nearby was burned down when the FBI suspected it of being a hideout for Japanese spies signalling submarines off the coast. *A-3* (see also Skaggs Island)

HIPPIE HOLLOW is a cluster of houses at the sharp turn on Warm Springs Road, about three-quarters of a mile from Arnold Drive in Glen Ellen. No doubt the name refers to inhabitants of the spot in the 1960s and '70s. *B-2*

A KINGDOM FOR A SONG

HOEPPNER'S BRANCH is an old name for Agua Caliente Creek. In 1843, the first pianos arrived in California, brought around Cape Horn by Captain Stephen Smith. Smith sold one of them in Los Angeles and another in Monterey. The third was purchased by General Vallejo. There was only one problem~no one within fifty miles of Sonoma knew how to play the instrument, and so it sat silent for three years in the Vallejos' parlor.

One evening in the spring of 1846, a young German named Andres Hoeppner arrived at Sonoma. The General urged him to spend the night at the Vallejo home. Hoeppner, a musician, was delighted to discover the piano and entertained his host and family with his playing. Before the night was over, Vallejo and Hoeppner had signed a contract: Hoeppner agreed to teach the family to play the piano with "all the science of the art" for at least five years. At the end of that time, Vallejo would give the musician title to over 2000 acres of land at *"agua caliente,"* which included present-day Agua Caliente Creek.

By August of 1850, Vallejo agreed that Hoeppner had fulfilled his obligation and deeded the land to him. Unfortunately, the young German did not get to enjoy the fruits of his labor for very long; he soon disappeared and his property was claimed by a number of squatters and claim jumpers. *C-3*

HOGBACK MOUNTAIN, in the Mayacamas between Napa and Sonoma Valleys, with its sharp crest and steep sides, resembles . . . what else? The back of a hog. *C-3*

HOOD MOUNTAIN is named after William Hood, a Scotsman who left home in his late teens to travel the world. In 1846 he climbed this peak and gazing down on Sonoma Valley, vowed to return when he'd made his fortune and own the land at the foot of the mountain. Hood realized his dream just four years later when he and his partner William Petit, a San Francisco merchant, purchased the Rancho Guilucos from John Wilson for $13,000, or 70 cents an acre.

By 1858, Hood had bought out his partner and using Indian labor to make fired bricks, built a residence on the property. He also planted 200 acres of grapes and built a three-story winery. His wife ended up running the wine operation, becoming one of three "lady winemakers" in the area in the 1880s. In the wake of the gold rush, many Americans squatted on Hood's land. In an effort to keep them off, Hood fenced and plowed large parts of his ranch. Even so, he lost nine-tenths of his property to his unwelcome neighbors. Hood died in 1903, aged eighty-four.

Hood Mountain was originally called Mount Hood. When word reached Oregon, home of a much taller peak by that name, there was a protest, and the name of the Sonoma Valley landmark switched to Hood Mountain. *A-1*
(see also Glen Ellen, Gunsight Rock & Guilicos)

THE CHECKERED CAREER OF "FIGHTING JOE"

HOOKER CREEK is named for Joseph Hooker, second in command of Sonoma's U.S. Army garrison from 1849 to '51. A West Point graduate, Hooker fought in the Mexican War. He was considered the best looking man in the U.S. Army, known by Mexican senoritas as *El Capitan Hermoso*, The Handsome Captain.

While stationed in Sonoma, Hooker supplemented his income by selling firewood and hay to the Army at double the price he was charged by local farmers. When the price gouging was discovered, Hooker was forced to resign his commission. As a civilian, Hooker purchased 550 acres of the Agua Caliente land grant, built a house of finished lumber that had come around the Horn, and briefly settled down to a farmer's life. In 1853 he was elected overseer of the county roads. Soon afterwards, he ran for state assemblyman on the Democratic ticket against James Bennett on the Settlers' ticket. After a bitter campaign, the election resulted in a tie vote; Hooker lost the runoff election by thirteen votes.

When the Civil War began, Hooker's offer of service to the Union was grudgingly accepted. Vigourous leadership in the field earned him the nickname "Fighting Joe," and he quickly rose to the rank of Major General. In January 1863, he was promoted to Commander of the Army of the Potomac. A seesawing record of defeats and victories in battle was often blamed on Hooker's overconfidence. When he lost to a Confederate force half the size of his own at Chancellorsville that June, "Fighting Joe" was relieved of his command.

At least two stories connect the term "hooker" to "Fighting Joe": One version says that the prostitutes he allowed to follow his army were nicknamed "Hooker's Ladies," later shortened to "Hooker's." Another story attributes the coining of the word to an incident in Sonoma when two new recruits asked if there were any loose women about. When the other soldiers said "no," the recruits inquired about two likely looking females they'd seen hanging around Army headquarters. "How about those two girls?" they asked. "They're Hooker's," was the reply. *C-3*

(see also Bear Creek & Bennett Mountain)

HUDSON'S CORNER was an old name for the northeast corner of the Sonoma Plaza. In the 1850s a building on First Street East was inhabited by Sam Hudson, his wife and their twenty-two children. Hudson was a ragpicker (today he'd be called a dumpster-diver), somehow supporting his huge family by picking up rags and junk and selling them. Frightened by the old man's grisly appearance, the kids of Sonoma would dare each other to approach Hudson and ask, "How's business?" To which he invariably replied, "Picking up." *Not on map*

HUICHICA is probably a hispanicized version of Hu'tci, the name of a Miwok village near the plaza. The name has been attached to a rancho, a creek, a valley and a school, all east of the town of Sonoma. Visiting this area in 1823, Father Jose Altimira said: "[We] saw 2 or 300 head of female elk. This species is much in abundance in all this land . . . as are also the antelope and deer." *C-4*

> (see also Hu'tci)

HU'TCI, sometimes spelled *Huchi,* was a Miwok village near the present-day Sonoma plaza. *C-4*

> (see also Huichica; see Sonoma for a possible meaning of Hu'tci)

KENWOOD BY ANY OTHER NAME

KENWOOD has two stories about its name. Like El Verano, the town sprang up with the arrival of the railroad. In 1887, the Sonoma Land & Improvement Company, which owned the property, laid out lots, anticipating the arrival of trains the following year. The infant community tried on several names: Rohrerville, for one of the owners of the Land Company; Los Guilicos, the title of the original Mexican land grant in the area; and then, when William Hood, the owner of the grant, objected, the name was altered slightly to South Los Guilicos.

A number of townspeople still weren't happy, grumbling that Guilicos was hard to pronounce. Around 1895 a vote was taken to change the name again. One story says that Kenwood won because many of the settlers had come from Kenwood, Illinois. Another traces the choice to the fact that many landowners in the area were from old English families and familiar with a London landmark known as the "Kenwood House." Perhaps both accounts are true and Kenwood stuck because it pleased people of different backgrounds. *B-2*

> (see also Guilicos)

KOHLER CREEK is a seasonal stream that flows from the lake at Jack London State Park through the vineyard below. The name comes from a German musician who, with his partner Frohling, fled the German revolution of 1848. Arriving in San Francisco with almost nothing, they established California's first wine-marketing business. To make ends meet while their enterprise grew, they played concerts of Mozart, Beethoven and Hayden to crowds of miners, sailors and other tough characters. Unable to afford a horse and wagon, Kohler made the first deliveries on foot, carrying the wine in a basket. In the 1850s they purchased property on Sonoma Mountain, planted a vineyard and introduced German techniques to California winemaking. By 1860 their business had grown so large they opened a branch office in New York City. Always involved in civic affairs, Kohler eventually became director of San Franciso's cable car system. *B-2*

LAC: " A place called '*Lac*' by the Indians" is mentioned in a petition for a land grant of the same name in 1844. *Lok* is the Wappo word for "goose." In Bodega Miwok, *laka* means "to be dry," and *lakko* is "to be thirsty." The Mexicans named the streambed running through this area *Arroyo Seco*, or "Dry Creek." *C-3*

THE WEEPING MOUNTAIN

LACHRYMA MONTIS, or "Tear of the Mountain" in Latin, was General Vallejo's name for both the spring on his estate and the estate itself. Some believe this is a translation of *Chiucuyem*, the Miwok name for the spring. Vallejo's grandson, Richard Emparan, used to tell a story that he said his grandfather either learned from the Indians or made up himself:

"A brave Indian chief who gained great fame as a warrior and leader of his tribe became enamored of a beautiful Indian maiden, and was about to make her his bride. Then a quarrel took place and parted the lovers. The broken-hearted maiden threw herself on the ground and shed bountiful tears, thus creating the beautiful spring which the Indians called 'Chiucuyem'."

Another version of the tale has the lovers committing a Romeo and Juliet style double suicide: The maiden throws herself into the spring. When her lover returns, he is so overcome with anguish at losing his sweetheart that he casts himself into the water and also drowns. Joined in death, their bitter tears turn sweet with joy, to pour happily down the mountainside.

The springs of Lachryma Montis produce about 750,000 gallons of fresh water a day. Vallejo piped the water into town and for many years supplied the residents of Sonoma with most of their drinking water. Though long believed inexhaustible, the springs have dried up at least once, in 1947. *C-3*

(see also Chiucuyem)

LEDSON MARSH, in Annadel State Park, is named after Barker and Edna Ledson, who purchased the property in 1930 and raised cattle and hay. Lacking a year-round supply of water, they built the low dam which created Ledson Marsh. *A-2*

FISHING IN THE KITCHEN SINK

LEWIS CREEK is probably named after L.L. Lewis, husband of Levisa Carriger, one of Nicholas Carriger's daughters. Around the turn of the 20th century, Lewis formed the Yulupa Land and Water Company and built a spring-fed reservoir with a capacity of twenty million gallons. He hoped to compete with Vallejo's municipal water system, irrigate orange groves in El Verano and supply power. Large redwood flumes were built to Sonoma and El Verano. Unfortunately, the citrus crops did not do well, and the reservoir, which was built on fill, began to settle and crack. Things went from bad to worse when the company started getting complaints about small trout clogging their customers's faucets. By 1918 the reservoir had fallen apart completely. *B-4*
(see also Carriger Creek, Lachryma Montis & Yulupa)

LOCUST GROVE, in Schellville, was the name of a boarding school that took its name from an avenue of locust trees planted in the 1870s. The students, who came from as far away as Mexico, enjoyed bathing and fishing in Sonoma Creek, which ran next to the school. The director of the school, Mrs. Charles Lubeck, also took in a number of orphans.

Locust trees, also known as honey locusts because their sweet-scented flowers attract lots of bees, have been called "The Tree of the Pioneers." Requiring little care, they were often planted as boundary markers. The wood made excellent fence posts and sometimes even took root and grew. *C-5*

JACK LONDON STATE PARK encompasses the ranch on Sonoma Mountain in Glen Ellen where the famous writer lived from 1905 to 1916. London's short life was filled to the brim, from prospecting in the Klondike Gold Rush, to hunting seals off the coast of Japan, to managing his 1500-acre ranch. By the age of twenty-five he had established himself as a writer. Committing himself to putting down a thousand words a day, Jack cranked out an amazing quantity of work, eventually publishing 53 books. Still one of the most widely read authors in the world, his works have been translated into more than 70 languages. At his Beauty Ranch in Glen Ellen, London experimented with different farming techniques and toward the end of his life said he enjoyed ranching more than writing. He died here at the age of forty, of kidney failure. *A-3*
(see also Cowan Meadow, Deer Camp, Hayfields, May's Clearing, Pine Tree Meadow & Wolf House)

LOS GUILICOS, see **GUILICOS & KENWOOD**

MADRONE ROAD gets its name from Madrone Vineyard, owned by Eli Sheppard in the late 1800s. He named the property for all the madrones that grew there. Before settling in Sonoma Valley, Sheppard fought in the Civil War and was a diplomat to China. Madrone was also the name of a nearby railway stop. *B-3*

MAMMY PLEASANT'S CAVE, in a remote spot somewhere in the Mayacamas, recalls Mary Ellen Pleasant, who owned Beltane Ranch in the late 19th century. According to one story, she used the the cave for casting spells against her enemies, most of whom were San Francisco businessmen. Born a slave in New Orleans, she admitted knowledge of Voodoo ritual, which is a blend of Catholicism and West African religion. Whether she actually used this cave is open to question. With her white business partner and lover, Thomas Bell, she amassed a covert fortune assessed at thirty million dollars. When Bell died suddenly, Mary Ellen was accused of his murder, vilified in the press, and nicknamed "Mammy" by her enemies.

On the other side of the coin, Mary Ellen has been called "The Mother of Civil Rights in California." Arriving in San Francisco in the 1850s, she helped fugitive slaves and fought legal battles to get blacks the right to ride city streetcars. Returning to the east, she was actively involved in the underground railroad and gave John Brown money for his ill-fated revolt. Disguised as a jockey, she traveled around near Harper's Ferry, trying to rouse the slaves to revolt. A letter signed with her initials was found on Brown when he was arrested, but because of her poor handwriting it was read as W.E.P. and she was never implicated. Back in California after the Civil War, she waged a series of legal battles to win blacks the right to testify in court. One of her contemporaries said, "If she had been white and a man she would have been President." *Not on map*

(see also Beltane Ranch)

MAYACAMAS was a Wappo name for a village near Calistoga and may also have designated the southern tidal areas of Napa and Sonoma Valleys, meaning "Water Going Out Place." The name is now attached to the mountain range between these two valleys, which continues north all the way to Lake County. The original pronunciation was closer to *Meyahk'mah*, the apostrophe standing for a glottal stop similar to the one in the middle of "uh-oh." *B-1 & C-2*

MAXWELL PARK was once the site of John Maxwell's farm. John sold the property to his son George in 1887. George, who developed El Verano, deeded the land to a charitable trust in 1906, ensuring that the land could not be sold for his debts. A respected man of principle, his ideas about open space and land conservation were well ahead of his time.

When George left Sonoma to study soil conservation in Arizona, his daughter Ruth took over the estate. She kept the ranch running, milking cows and raising prunes, ducks, chickens, and horses. She also loved stray cats, which she kept on the second floor of her barn, which occupied the site where Lucky Market now stands.

The original trust declared that once the family no longer used the property, it would be made available "for the purpose of providing education in the garden and home crafts." The trust was declared invalid in 1976, and in 1987 the Sonoma City Council and the voters approved the construction of Maxwell Village Shopping Center along with preserving the rest of the property as Maxwell Park. *B-3*

(see also El Verano)

MAY'S CLEARING, in Jack London State Park, gets its name from a French woodcutter who lived there in the 19th century. *A-3*

(see also Embarcadero)

MCGILL'S LANDING was the name of the furthest downstream landing for the steamer *Sonoma* when tides were especially low. *C-5*

(see also Embarcadero)

MIDSHIPMAN POINT, at the southern end of the valley on San Pablo Bay, has obscure origins going back to the mid-19th century. A midshipman serves 'amidships', (the middle of the ship) and is an ensign-in-training, the Navy's lowest ranking commissioned officer. Perhaps there was some connection with the old Naval base at Mare Island, ten miles east at Vallejo. *C-6*

MISSION, see **SAN FRANCISCO SOLANO**

MOUNTAIN OF THE BURNING BIRD is said to be an old name for Bennett Mountain. Whether a translation of a Miwok, Pomo or Wappo name or one given by an early settler is unclear. Local lore says that during bad times native people burned a white bird in effigy on top of this peak. While no such ritual has been reported for local tribes, the Sierra Miwok (cultural relatives of Sonoma's Coast Miwoks) held a somewhat similar event. In September or October, they created effigies of departed friends and relatives and made gifts of food and baskets that the dead would need in the other world. A huge bonfire was lit on top of a hill or mountain and the gifts and effigies burned in a communal expression of grief. (There are surprising parallels here with *El Dia de los Muertos*, Mexico's Day of the Dead, as well as our own Halloween.) If such rites took place on Bennett Mountain they might have been misinterpreted by someone unfamiliar with native culture. The Wappos did make effigies of owls and hawks, though there is no record of them being burned or associated with mourning. *A-2*
(see also Bennett Mountain & Yulupa)

NAPA STREET was *Calle Napa* in Mexican times because it was the beginning of the trail to Napa. After California became an American possession, *Calle Napa* was renamed United States Street. Later it became Napa Street, the English version of its original name. One source says *napa* is a Pomo word meaning "harpoon point." Another says *napa* means "bear doctor." ***Not on map***

NATHANSON CREEK gets its name from a pioneer family who lived in the hills northeast of Sonoma, along this creek. *C-3*
(see story below)

A HARD JOURNEY TO SONOMA

In February 1849, German newlyweds Martin and Dorothea Nathanson boarded the *Steinberger* in Hamburg, bound for California. After a whirlwind courtship, and the two teenagers had been married on Dorothea's sixteenth birthday. When Martin's family promptly disowned him, Dorothea's father agreed to finance a journey to America, where they hoped to make a fresh start.

On the way around Cape Horn, the ship was badly damaged by several storms and barely made it to the port of Valparaiso, Chile. There, Dorothea gave birth to their first child, a girl named Caroline. For three weeks she nursed her newborn while the *Steinberger* lay at anchor for repairs, but on the first night back at sea, Caroline died. Dorothea begged the captain to return to port so she could bury her child on solid ground, but the ship was already long overdue and he refused. Taking off the gold engagement ring Martin had given her, she pressed it into the hand of a sailor and asked him to retrieve the wedding veil from her trunk in the ship's hold. When he returned, she sewed Caroline's body in it and sat through the night, her baby in her arms. At dawn, while the captain read the burial service, Dorothea walked to the rail and dropped Caroline's remains overboard. The little bundle spun a few times in the wake of the ship and disappeared beneath the waves. Overwhelmed with grief, Dorothea fainted and crumpled to the deck.

After nine months, the *Steinberger* finally reached San Francisco in December. Dorothea was not yet seventeen. She and Martin opened a restaurant right on the water; they could see the bay through the cracks in the floorboards. Women were scarce in gold rush San Francisco and Martin grew jealous of the customers flirting with his wife. After accusing Dorothea of flirting back, he decided the only solution was for the two of them to leave town.

The couple moved to Sonoma in 1851, at first sharing Casa Grande with the Vallejos while the General waited for his new home at Lachryma Montis to be finished. Martin ended up purchasing a lot from Vallejo, and using surplus lumber from the newly completed Methodist church, built a grocery store (now known as the Toscano Hotel) next to the Barracks. Eventually the family homesteaded a farm east of town, on the banks of the creek that now bears their name. Martin and Dorothea went on to have seven more children, all of whom reached adulthood.

MOUNT NEBO, a former name for Bismarck Knob, was named for the mountain from which Moses saw the Promised Land: "And Moses went up from the plains of Moab to Mount Nebo, to the top of Pisgah . . ." *C-2*

Deuteronomy 34:1

(see also Bismarck Knob & Mount Pisgah)

NEW SAN FRANCISCO, see **PULPULA**

NORFOLK was the original name of Wingo. The name probably leapfrogged from Norfolk, England, a county on the North Sea, to the seaport of Norfolk, Virginia, and then to Sonoma Valley, where its days as a port have long since passed.

Norfolk was the terminus for the valley's first railroad, the Prismodial Line, built in the 1870s. At that time, Norfolk had a warehouse, passenger depot and agent's quarters. Trains shuttled four miles to Schellville, running on

a specially shaped single wooden rail. Plans to extend the line to Santa Rosa were never realized and within four years this unusual railway was defunct. *C-5*
(see also Wingo)

NUNNS CANYON is named after homesteader Hugh Nunn. By the 1860s all the good land on the floor of Sonoma Valley had been claimed, so the second wave of immigrants (predominantly Scotch, Irish and German) headed for the hills. A number of settlers homesteaded along Calabazas Creek, including Nunn in 1862. Access was by a dangerous winding road that crossed back and forth over the creek on log bridges; several people died on it before the route was abandoned in the 1920s. During the rainy season it was too muddy for a horse and cart, and homesteaders like Nunn had to walk to Glen Ellen for supplies. Hugh would make the return journey of three or four uphill miles, lugging a 100-pound sack of flour on his back.

The Nunns Canyon Fire of September, 1964 consumed 10,000 acres in three days, burning north to Adobe Canyon and south to Agua Caliente. *B-2*
(see also Calabazas Creek)

OONA-PA'IS was the Miwok name for Sonoma Mountain. *Pa'is* means "hill" or "mountain." *Oona* does not appear in any Miwok dictionaries, but the sound is very close to *oonoo*, the word for buckeye nut. There are extensive groves of buckeye on the upper slopes of the mountain, forming pure stands reminiscent of orchards. So the original meaning may have been "Buckeye Mountain." *A-3*
(see story below)

WHERE THE WORLD BEGAN

The world was made by O-ye the Coyote-man. The earth was covered with water. The only thing that showed above the water was the very top of Oona-pa'is.

In the beginning O-ye came on a raft from the west, from across the ocean. His raft was a mat of tules and split sticks; it was long and narrow. O-ye landed on top of Oona-pa'is and threw his mat out over the water ~ the long way north and south, the narrow way east and west; the middle rested on top of the peak. That was the beginning of the world and the world is still long and narrow like a mat ~ the long way north and south, the narrow way east and west.

When O-ye was sitting alone on top of Oona-pa'is and all the rest of the world was covered with water, he saw a feather floating toward him, blown by the wind from the west–the direction from which he himself had come. He asked the feather, "Who are you?"

The feather made no reply.

He then told the feather about his family and all his relatives. When he came to mention Wek-wek, his grandson, the feather leapt out of the water and said, "I am Wek-wek, your grandson."

O-ye the Coyote-man was glad, and they talked together.

Every day O-ye noticed Ko-to-lah the Frog-Woman sitting near him. Every time he saw her he reached out his hand and tried to catch her, but she always jumped into the water and escaped.

After four days the water began to go down, leaving more land on top of the mountain, so that Ko-to-lah had to make several leaps to reach the water. This gave O-ye the advantage and he ran after her and caught her. When he had caught her he was surprised to find that she was his own wife from over the ocean. Then he was glad.

When the water went down the land was dry. O-ye planted the buckeye and elderberry and oak trees, and all the other kinds of trees, and also bushes and grasses, all at the same time. But there were no people and he and Wek-wek wanted people. Then O-ye took a quantity of feathers of different kinds and packed them up to the top of Oona-pa'is and threw them up into the air and the wind carried them off and scattered them all over the country and they turned into people, and the next day there were people all over the land.

(In another version, O-ye makes the feathers into four bundles and sets them in the ground at four different places. The next morning all had turned into people, each bundle becoming a distinct tribe, speaking an entirely different language.)

from *Dawn of the World*, as told to C. Hart Merriam
by a Coast Miwok elder
in 1908.

PANSY VALLEY is an area of the original Buena Vista vineyard. The first Vintage Festival, a pageant along classical lines was held here. The origin of Pansy Valley's name is unknown. *C-4*

(see also Haraszthy Creek)

PETALUMA originally referred to a Miwok village west of Sonoma Valley, near the modern town of the same name. General Vallejo borrowed the name for his Rancho Petaluma, whose eastern border was along Sonoma Creek. Vallejo's translation of Petaluma as "Oh Fair Vale" is of doubtful authenticity. Tom Smith, a Miwok elder interviewed in the 1930s, said *petaluma* meant "back." A slightly different translation is "flat back", referring to the shape of the hills in the area, particularly Sonoma Mountain. ***Not on map***

PINE TREE MEADOW, in Jack London State Park, gets its name from a very large ponderosa pine that grows there, said to be the only one on Sonoma Mountain. *A-3*

MOUNT PISGAH, near the top of Moon Mountain Road, gets its name from the Hebrew *pisgah*, meaning peak or summit, the place from which Moses saw the Promised Land:

"Let me go over, I pray, and see the good land beyond the Jordan, that goodly hill country, and Lebanon. And the Lord said to me, 'Go to the top of Pisgah, and lift your eyes westward and northward and southward and eastward, and behold it with your eyes, for you shall not go over the Jordan. But charge Joshua, and encourage and strengthen him; for he shall go over and take possession of that good land.' " *C-3*

adapted from *Deuteronomy 3:27*

(see also Glen Ellen & Mount Nebo)

TIME TRAVELING ON THE PLAZA

THE PLAZA was surveyed by General Vallejo and his friend William Richardson in the summer of 1835, soon after the Pueblo of Sonoma was established. Vallejo and Richardson extended the dirt street in front of the mission to the west and the one in front of the guardhouse to the south, establishing the north and east sides of the plaza. From this beginning, the rest of the square was laid out with the idea that the pueblo's remaining streets could be surveyed as needed.

continued

Besides the raising of the Bear Flag in 1846, Sonoma's plaza has seen many changes through the years:

In the 1840s, Lieutenant Edwin Bryant described the plaza as an open area whose "only ornaments were numerous skulls and dislocated skeletons of beef cattle, and with these ghastly remains the ground was strewn."

In the 1850s the plaza was pockmarked with large holes excavated to make adobe bricks for houses and other buildings. During the rainy season, these holes filled with water, providing a refuge for wild ducks. Wild mustangs were sometimes brought to the plaza and young men challenged each other to ride them. "Dog and coon" fights were common, the men putting down large bets on their dogs. Most of the time the racoons whipped the dogs.

Visitors to the plaza in the 1860s sometimes heard the picking of Chinese banjos and musical kites strung with rubber bands buzzing in the wind. The plaza was completely open in those days, with no trees or buildings.

By 1880, a train station occupied the north side of the square, while on the south side an octagonal pavilion was being constructed to serve as Sonoma's municipal headquarters. A fence surrounded the plaza, and a few trees had been planted.

In the 1890s, the train station was dismantled and a two-cell city jail was constructed. A bicycle track built by the Sonoma Bicycle Club was the scene of many races until a violent fight broke out among cycling enthusiasts and the City Council ordered the track abandoned.

The early years of the 20th century saw the plaza beginning to take its current form. The Sonoma Valley Women's Club put in paths, benches and fountains. Plagued by striking workers and the 1906 earthquake, work on City Hall was finally completed in 1908 and dedicated with a parade, races, concerts and a barbecue. To keep all the merchants happy, the building was designed to look identical from all four sides. Andrew Carnegie donated $6000 to build a public library on the plaza's east side, which was completed in 1913 (now home to the Sonoma Valley Visitor's Bureau). That same year, the California Legislature allocated money for a Bear Flag monument and the huge rock that serves as a pedestal for the statue was moved from the northern end of First Street West. ***Not on map***

(see also First Street East, First Street West, Hudson's Corner, Napa Street & Spain Street)

POPPE'S LANDING was one place where travelers arrived and departed by water in the latter part of the 19th century. Downstream from the Embarcadero, it served as a port for Sonoma when tides were too low to permit navigation further upstream. It was located in Schellville on the ranch of J.A. Poppe, a

German immigrant who came to Sonoma around 1849. With picks and shovels, Chinese laborers built a causeway across the marshes to the landing. *C-5*
(see also China Slough, Embarcadero, Pulpula & Wingo)

PULPULA was a Miwok village in the Schellville area, in the vicinity of present-day Cline Cellars. A likely translation is "ponds": *polpol* means "lake" or "pond" in Lake Miwok. Father Jose Altimira, visiting the site in 1823, noted: "for 500 *varas* [one-quarter mile] of distance, there are small ponds with small permanent springs of sweet water, abundant and very clear which come out between rocks."

J.A. Poppe noted six ponds in the area when he settled there in 1852. One was a hot spring that he piped into a bathhouse. A band of "friendly Indians" was still living there at that time. *C-5*

THE NEW SAN FRANCISCO

Pulpula was the original site chosen for the Sonoma Mission. After the soldiers in his party raised a 20-foot high cross and discharged a musket volley, Father Jose Altimira sang hymns, celebrated Mass and proclaimed the place to be "The New San Francisco." Just twelve days later he changed his mind and moved the mission to its present location, saying "the west winds blew too hard at Pulpula."

It was also at Pulpula that Mariano Vallejo camped upon his arrival in Sonoma Valley in 1834, with thirty colonists for the newly founded pueblo. Depending on which account you believe, from several hundred to 11,000 natives gathered here for a week of feasting, dancing, games and gift-giving as the leaders of local tribes met and signed treaties with the new representative of the Mexican govenment.
(see also Poppe's Landing, San Francisco Solano & Wingo)

QALEQOCI CREEK, which runs through Ernie Smith Park in El Verano, was named by twelve-year-old Garrett Smith during Sonoma Valley's first Creek Day in 1997. Garrett's suggestion of *qaleqoci*, a Kashaya Pomo word for the long net-like lichen which hang from the park's oak trees, was chosen as the winner of a creek-naming competition. By pure coincidence, Ernie Smith, the park's namesake, was Garrett's great-grandfather.

This type of lichen, sometimes erroneously called "Spanish Moss," only grows in unpolluted areas and is considered an indicator of good air quality. Deer enjoy this lichen after the first autumn rains cause many of them to fall to the ground. *B-3*

RATTLESNAKE CREEK is in Sugarloaf Ridge State Park. Keep your eyes peeled if you go hiking here; there's an abundance of this poisonous snake in the area. *B-1*

RED MOUNTAIN, in Sugarloaf Ridge State Park, is covered with chamise, a type of chaparral. In late summer this plants darkens to russet, creating a ruddy mosaic on the mountain's slopes. *B-1*

RAILROAD SLOUGH, see **NORFOLK, SCHELLVILLE & WINGO** for the history of railroads in this area. *C-5*

STILL RUNNING FROM THE PAST

RODGERS CREEK should really be called Kissane Creek, for the man it is named after lived at Temelec Hall under a false name for twenty-five years:

William Kissane was a notorious criminal whose crimes included a scam where he insured a ship and its cargo, then set the vessel on fire and collected the money. Sixteen passengers never made it back to shore alive. He also swindled banks in New York and was an accomplished forger. Though twice convicted, he managed to escape the law both times.

After his second escape, Kissane took an assumed name and joined William Walker's 1856 expedition to Nicaragua, which overthrew the government of that country. Walker became president and appointed his cronies to various powerful positions. For eight months Kissane had control of the country's finances and used his power to seize property and hold the wives and children of prominent Nicaraguans for ransom. Eventually, someone from the States recognized Kissane, greeting him by name on the street. Soon afterwards that unlucky individual was found murdered by unknown assailants. Kissane had a death notice for himself printed in a Nicaraguan newspaper and fled to China, where he took part in the Taiping Rebellion.

Back in the Americas, Kissane acquired a fortune as a prospector (or so he said) in the gold fields of British Columbia and California. With this wealth, he bought Temelec Hall in 1863 under the alias of Colonel William K.

Rodgers. (Kissane had held the rank of Colonel in Nicaragua) There he and his wife Elizabeth raised eight children and became respected members of the community.

A strange twist of fate finally revealed Rodgers' true identity. In 1879, former President Grant came to California on tour. Looking for a suitable overnight spot in Sonoma Valley, his Secret Service agents chose Temelec Hall. Rodgers, fearing someone in Grant's party might recognize him, declined, claiming he didn't have enough space. Rodgers' refusal aroused suspicion and an investigation was begun. It took the authorities years to put all the puzzle pieces together; finally, in 1890, Kissane was brought to trial for his crimes. Once more he escaped punishment, saved by good lawyers and the statute of limitations. But the experience of being revealed for who he was left Kissane a broken man. In 1893 he sold Temelec to pay his debts. *B-4*

(see also Temelec)

ROHRERVILLE, see **KENWOOD**

ANOTHER SAN FRANCISCO

MISSION SAN FRANCISCO SOLANO, the title chosen for Sonoma's mission, was not the name Father Jose Altimira originally wanted, and reflects a power struggle between church and state in early California:

Arriving in California in 1821, young Altimira was appalled by the horrible conditions at Mission San Francisco de Asis. The Indian neophytes struggling to survive on the fog-shrouded sand dunes were dying in such numbers that Mission San Rafael, had been established as a "hospital mission" across the bay (the climate was milder there). For several years there had been talk among church authorities about moving Mission San Francisco itself to a better spot.

Growing impatient with the older padres, Altimira wrote a letter to the *diputacion*, California's six-member territorial legislature. He proposed transferring both Mission San Rafael and Mission San Francisco to a single new location north of the Bay. Also concerned with checking the Russian incursion at Fort Ross, the *diputacion* gave his plan their full support, though they had no legal authority in the matter. Without waiting for permission from his religious superiors, Altimira made an expedition to the North Bay and established a mission at Sonoma, calling it "The New San Francisco."

Outraged by this challenge to their authority, the church fathers ordered a halt to all work on the new mission. Although Altimira obeyed, he sent an angry letter to his friend, Governor Luis Arguello, accusing the padres of aiding "the office of Satan by throwing obstacles in the way of a great enterprise."

Father Vicente Sarria, president of the missions, also wrote an impassioned letter to the Governor, explaining the church's position and comparing Altimira to England's Henry the Eighth. "What a labyrinth!" he wrote. "Political authorities assuming the functions of a bishop."

Governor Arguello replied that because the Sonoma mission had already been established, it would continue as a military post. He threatened to refer the matter to the central government in Mexico if Altimira was not allowed to continue his work.

Several more heated letters were exchanged before a compromise was finally reached. The governor and the church agreed to let the San Francisco and San Rafael Missions remain where they were, while permitting Altimira to continue with the establishment of the mission at Sonoma. The new mission would not be "The New San Francisco" that he envisioned, but instead would be named after another San Francisco~San Francisco Solano, the patron saint of Peru. ***Not on map***

San Francisco Solano, born in 1549 to an aristocratic family in southern Spain, was named for Saint Francis of Assisi. Fond of music, he played the violin and liked to sing. At the age of twenty he joined a Franciscan monastery. Seven years later he was ordained into the priesthood. His first miracle was to cure a small boy who was covered with running sores. Minutes after Francisco touched him, the sores dried up. Another time, a cripple with badly ulcerated legs was instantly healed when Francisco kissed his feet.

At the age of forty, Francisco sailed to South America. Stopping to rest on a journey from Lima, Peru to establish a mission in the Andes, he pulled out his violin and began to play. A local Indian chief was watching from the bushes, and grew so enraptured by the music that he came out of hiding. The two men became friends, and soon the chief and his whole tribe were converted to Christianity. Returning to Lima, Francisco became famous for fiery sermons and more miracles. He died there in 1610, after twenty-one years in South America.

(see also Pulpula & Schocken Hill)

SONOMA'S ST. LOUIS

SAN LUIS, later changed to St. Louis, was the village that sprang up around Sonoma's Embarcadero. The name's origin is unknown. Englishman Frank Marryat gave this description of the place in April, 1851:

"Here are three houses, which represent the town of San Luis; opposite the town some fishing boats lay at anchor, and in one of these I bargained for a passage to San Francisco, in company with eight live bullocks, that were now lying on the strand, bound neck and heels together, moaning piteously, as if impatient to get to the butcher's and have it all over. With the exception of the owners of the three houses, the population of San Luis was a particularly floating one, being represented for the most part by crews of the fishing smacks, of which there were at times a great number in port.

From the centre house there proceeded the sound of a fiddle, and it became evident that the floating population had there assembled to while away the hours until the tide served to enable the boats to leave. I entered the house and found it to consist of a store and drinking-shop combined, filled, as I had anticipated, by the men belonging to the boats, who, already half drunk, were tossing off champagne, out of tin pannikins, and drinking to a speedy voyage across the bay. The proprietor of the establishment was an Englishman, one of those plump, rosy-cheeked, good-natured-looking fellows that attract the eye at once, and whose smile is sympathetic. I shall call him Ramsey. When Ramsey came up to San Francisco with a cargo of flour, in the expectation of making a fortune; and when he determined on taking the flour up the River Sacramento, and the flour was caught in a squall in the bay and went down, Ramsey found that he had done a very foolish thing. However, all smiles and good-humour, he took the grog-shop and store at San Luis, where I found him.

I started at last, with fair wind and tide, for San Francisco, in a small yawl, with a crew of three men, who were not only half-drunk, but were about the greatest lubbers that ever went afloat. Before we reached the mouth of the creek, they managed to run the boat on the bank, where the ebb tide soon left us high and dry. While waiting for the flood tide to take us off, we are spitefully pelting, out of a bag of beans, the muddy little crabs that surround our stranded bark. The flood-tide is coming in, I take a parting shot at a little crab that has not taken his eyes off me since we arrived, and wonders I suppose, why I don't pelt one of my own size, and gliding off our mud bank, we make sail for San Francisco." *C-5*

adapted from *North Bay Journal & Visits to San Francisco*
(see also Embarcadero)

SCHELLVILLE: Early landowner Theodore Schell gained a small measure of immortality when the Sonoma Valley Railroad built a station near his property in 1879 and called it Schellville, the name still used for this vaguely defined area south of Sonoma. A Forty-niner, Schell settled on his 1000-acre ranch in 1860.

When another railroad, the Southern Pacific, laid tracks through the same area in 1887, they spelled their station Shellville. Around this time a townsite was laid out and lots were advertised in the *Schellville Ray*, the local

newspaper. At the junction of two railroads, the road to Sonoma, and close to
the wharves at Embarcadero, Schellville was expected to become a large and
prosperous town. For awhile it boasted several hotels, a bowling alley,
lumberyard, general store, its own post office and school. But around the turn
of the century, Schellville's prospects also took a turn. As Sonoma Creek filled
with mud, larger vessels could no longer reach Embarcadero and the landing
moved downstream. Left high and dry, Schellville's dream of becoming a town
slowly faded away. *C5*
(see also Embarcadero, Norfolk & Wingo)

SCHOCKEN HILL is named for Solomon Schocken, who came to Sonoma in 1873.
His general store was located on the plaza, in the old Barracks. Around 1880 he
opened a cobblestone quarry on the hill.   Blockmakers were paid by the piece,
earning six to seven dollars a day to carve out the basalt cobblestones, which
were shipped from Embarcadero on schooners. In the twenty years Schocken
owned the business, millions of blocks from Sonoma were used for paving
streets all over northern California, including San Francisco and Sacramento.
Demand for the blocks declined in the early twentieth century as asphalt began
to replace cobblestones. *C3*
(see also Battery Hill & the story below)

JERUSALEM IN SONOMA

When Solomon Schocken opened his store on the plaza, his reduced rates drew
throngs of customers. Established merchants resented his thriving business, which was
cutting heavily into their profits. When they had no success underselling him, they dug
up an obscure law requiring businesses to close on the sabbath and notified the
authorities that Schocken was doing business on Sundays. Schocken was arrested and
hauled in front of the Justice of the Peace, who fined him ten dollars.

Unfazed, Schocken closed his store on the next Jewish Sabbath of Saturday, but
opened again on Sunday. Again he was brought before the Justice of the Peace, where he
pleaded that he *had* kept the Sabbath as decreed by his religion. The words were barely
out of his mouth when the Justice roared, "Damn you! Do you wish to transplant
Jerusalem to Sonoma? Mr. Clerk, please collect a fine of twenty-five dollars from the
prisoner, and if he ever again be brought before me on a charge of this kind, he shall be
sent to prison."

Schocken never again opened on Sunday, but he did receive some poetic justice
when he bought the Sonoma Mission property. He used the chapel for a warehouse,

filling it with hay, liquor, beer and other merchandise. One observer described it as a "saloon, a barn and a henhouse all in one." Schocken eventually sold the mission property to William Randolph Hearst, who deeded it to the state as a Historic Landmark.

SEARS POINT gets its name from pioneer Franklin Sears, a blacksmith by trade. Born in Indiana in 1817, Sears spent most of his childhood in Missouri. At the age of twenty-seven he set out for Oregon with a rifle, a mule, a dollar fifty in cash, and his friend Granville Swift, who along the way headed south to California. One winter in Oregon was enough for Sears. He got so sick of the rain that one morning he suddenly announced, "I'm going to California." Joining up with his friend again at Sutter's Fort, Sears hunted deer and elk in the Central Valley. When the Mexican War broke out, Sears volunteered for the army and earned the title "Hero of San Pasquale." His buckskin shirt was riddled by seven bullets in that battle, of which he was one of the few American survivors.

In 1851, Sears married Swift's sister Margaret and the couple moved onto a 600-acre ranch south of Sonoma, where they built a house of hand-hewn redwood. Sears Point got its name when Sears and Swift purchased 15,000 acres of land stretching from Sears Point to Lakeville. In old age, Sears sometimes wandered off aimlessly into the hills. When his absence was discovered, the local fire bell would ring and Sears' friends and neighbors would gather to search the hills until he was found. *C-6*

(see also Temelec & the story below)

CLOTH FOR THE BEAR FLAG

After traveling for months in a covered wagon, Franklin Sears' brother John and his wife arrived in Sonoma on June 14, 1846, the day of the Bear Flag Rebellion. Wanting to create a flag for themselves, several of the *Osos*, or Bear Men, knocked on Mrs. Sears' door to see if she had any cloth. Roused from sleep, Mrs. Sears tore three yards from a bolt of homespun muslin she had brought with her all the way from Missouri and gave it to them. According to one account, an old sailor named Matthews stole his wife's petticoat off the clothesline to serve as the red stripe across the bottom of the flag, which was sewn onto Mrs. Sears' muslin.

When the Stars and Stripes were hoisted over Sonoma just 25 days later, John Sears, now a lieutenant in the Bear Flag Army, was sad to see the Bear Flag come down.

continued

He said, "The American flag has come down too soon and all the work of the Bear Flaggers is lost." Like many *Osos*, he had hoped to see California become a Texas-style republic.

The lettering and artwork on the original Bear Flag were done by William Todd, who was Abraham Lincoln's nephew. One observer thought the bear looked more like a pig. (This sketch of the original Bear Flag was done from a photograph. The flag burned during the 1906 San Francisco earthquake.)

SECRET PASTURE, high in the Mayacamas southeast of Glen Ellen, is said to have been used by Joaquin Murrieta and his gang to pasture rustled cattle. To avoid detection, the outlaws sealed off the single entrance with brush after driving the cattle into the clearing.

Charles Justi, who ran the stage stop in Glen Ellen in those days, said Murrieta and some of his men once stopped by asking for a place to spend the night. Pretending not to recognize them, Justi put them up. The next morning they went peacefully on their way. Another time, Justi discovered some of his cattle missing and set off to locate the rumored "Secret Pasture." After a difficult scramble up the steep mountainside, he found the place. Sure enough, the pasture held a big herd of rustled cattle, including Justi's. Because of the danger involved, Justi decided to leave his animals where they were and never did recover them. *B-2*

(see story below)

JOAQUIN THE BANDIT & THREE-FINGERED JACK

Whether Joaquin Murrieta and his men *really* visited Sonoma Valley is open to question. During the early 1850s, when the Murrieta legend was born, reports of his presence came from many parts of the state. Numerous crimes probably committed by others were attributed to him. According to one source, there were four independent gangs coordinating efforts, and among them were several Joaquins. *El Famoso*, as the most famous Joaquin was nicknamed, was a tall, blond Mexican who came to California during the gold rush. He was fluent enough in English to pass for an American.

Though *El Famoso* did commit several acts of violence (against miners who had murdered members of his family) and may have occasionally rustled cows, his principal activity was running horses to Mexico. At a rendevous point near Mount Diablo, he and his men gathered wild mustangs (and some not-so-wild horses) and drove them in huge herds along an 800-mile trail to Sonora, Mexico. The *Tres Dedos* gang headed by Three-Fingered Jack did commit wholesale acts of robbery and murder, and because of this were considered outcast by the other three gangs. Besides multiple Joaquins, there were at least two "Three-Fingered Jacks," Bernardino Garcia and Manuel Duarte. Garcia *did* spend time in Sonoma. One source says his nickname was actually "Four-Fingered Jack", which may account for the confusion.

Joaquin Murrieta as he is believed to have appeared in the 1850s

The California Rangers claim to have killed Joaquin and Three-Fingered Jack in 1853 at a remote spot south of San Francisco. They cut off Joaquin's head and Three-Fingered Jack's hand as proof of their deed. Because the head did not match authentic descriptions of *El Famoso's* appearance, some believe he never was apprehended. The head and hand were preserved in alcohol, placed in jars, and put on display in San Francisco. They disappeared during the 1906 earthquake and fire.

(see also Fowler Creek)

SKAGGS ISLAND is named for M.B. Skaggs, the founder of Safeway and Payless stores. The U.S. Navy used it as a radio relay station from the outbreak of World War II until 1993, when the base was closed.

Originally an expanse of salt marsh bordered by tidal sloughs, the island was purchased in 1878 by the Pacific Reclamation Company as part of a 10,000-acre tract that included Tubbs Island and four other islands. The plan was to convert the marshes into agriculturally productive land. At first, crews of Chinese laborers were employed to build levees around the islands with shovels and wheelbarrows. As it became apparent what a huge undertaking this was (Skaggs Island alone has 15 miles of shoreline), the owners of the company turned to mechanical power, utilizing dredges, specially built plows and steam-powered tractors.

By the First World War, the company was growing hay on the island to supply the Bay Area with horse feed. As late as 1923, San Francisco consumed 5,000 tons of hay a month to fuel its horsedrawn transportation. Within three years however, the city had become motorized, and the bottom fell out of the hay market. Soon afterwards the depression hit and the company was unable to answer its financial obligations. M.B. Skaggs offered to take over the indebtedness. By 1938, the Pacific Reclamation Company owed Skaggs a large sum of money and could no longer meets its financial commitments. In lieu of cash, the company deeded the island to Skaggs. Skaggs didn't really want the property and in 1940, he sold the island to the Navy. *C-6 & D-6*

SKY ROCK, on the ridge trail in Glen Ellen Regional Park, was named by local newspaper columnist Sylvia Crawford's family for her oldest son Schuyler, whose nickname is Sky. Good views of Sonoma Valley, the Mayacamas, and a broad expanse of sky make Sky Rock a doubly appropriate name for this spot. *B-2*

SOBRE VISTA, named by Maria Hooper, wife of Colonel Hooper, in the late 19th century, means "over look" in Spanish. The broad verandas of her home on Sonoma Mountain had a spectacular panorama of Sonoma Valley. *B-3*

THE MYSTERIOUS MEANING OF SONOMA

SONOMA   first appears in the written record in 1815 as *"Chucuines o Sonomas"* (Chiucuyems or Sonomas), a tribal name in mission baptismal lists. There are at least four stories about the name's origin and meaning:

"Valley of the Moon," the most well-known "translation" of Sonoma, probably originated with General Vallejo, who said *sono* meant 'moon' in Suisun, a language he learned from his friend, Chief Solano. Vallejo explained that as one travels through the valley at night, the full moon seems to rise and set several times over the eastern hills. (Almost all native place names in Sonoma Valley appear to derived from Coast Miwok rather than Suisun, the language of a tribe who lived in Napa Valley. Vallejo's creativity sometimes exceeded his accuracy when it came to translating native place names. See Petaluma)

Vallejo's son, Platon, gave what might be called the "Pinocchio Version" of Sonoma's meaning: Tomo, an Indian servant who spoke Suisun or a closely related language, told Platon that *sono* meant "nose." He said that long before the Mexicans came, a baby was born in the valley with a particularly large nose. As he grew, his nose grew with him. Eventually, he became chief of the tribe and his name was attached to the valley. Thus Sonoma means "The Land of Chief Big Nose."

Several sources point to what may be the most authentic interpretation: Theodore Kroeber, a famous California anthropologist of the early 20th century, noted that *-sonoma* is a common Wappo suffix often appearing at the end of village names. Examples are *Tekenansonoma* near Cobb Mountain, *Anakotasonoma* near Mount St. Helena, and *Nihlekt'sonoma* near Calistoga. Laura Somersal, the last fluent speaker of Wappo, who died in 1990, also thought Sonoma may have come from the Wappo and meant "abandoned camping place." This suggests the possibility that the Wappo, who some anthropologists believe have lived in this area for more than 10,000 years, may have occupied Sonoma Valley before being pushed out by the Miwok, who are thought to have arrived *only* about 3000 years ago.

Another version of local lore (often quoted by allergy sufferers) holds that Sonoma means "valley of sickness,"on account of all the hayfever caused by the area's abundant vegetation. Unlikely as it seems, there may be a thread of truth to this: The village in the vicinity of the Sonoma Plaza was called *Hu'tci*. No translation exists for this Sonoma Miwok word, but the sound is almost identical to *hotci*, which in Bodega Miwok means "sneeze." Say this word out loud and you'll hear something pretty close to "ACHOO"! *C-4*

(see also Huichica)

SONOMA MOUNTAIN, see **OONA-PA'IS & SONOMA**

SPAIN STREET was once *Calle Vallejo* (Vallejo Street), because it ran in front of *El Casa Grande*, General Vallejo's first house in Sonoma, which he built next to the Barracks. ***Not on map***
(see also The Plaza)

STAGE GULCH ROAD follows the old stagecoach route from Sonoma to Lakeville. Travelers would take the stage over the hills to Lakeville, get on a train for the short trip to Donahue Landing on the Petaluma River and from there journey by steam paddlewheeler across the bay to San Francisco. *B-5*

STEAMBOAT SLOUGH: see **STOFEN'S LANDING** for information about one of the steamboats that plied these waters. *C-5*

STOFEN'S LANDING got its name from two brothers, Captains Jack and Peter Stofen, who came to Embarcadero in 1863. Purchasing 190 acres, they went into business hauling freight and passengers between Sonoma Valley and San Francisco. With products from the valley increasing, their services were in great demand. Before long they owned four warehouses and a fleet of schooners and barges. In 1874 they built the *Sonoma*, a sternwheel steamer, which provided both passenger and freight service. A big crowd gathered at Stofen's Landing to celebrate her arrival from San Francisco on her maiden voyage.

The coming of the Sonoma Valley Railroad gave the Stofen brothers' enterprise a temporary setback. However, when fruit shippers complained that the quality of produce arriving by rail was not very good, the Stofens were in business again. One of the Stofen's ships, *The Gazelle* (designed by Peter), was the fastest sloop on the bay, winning the Master Mariner Association's regatta many years in a row. **C-5**

(see Embarcadero for a picture of the steamer *Sonoma*)

STUART CREEK is named after Charles and Mary Ellen Stuart, who settled in the Glen Ellen area in 1859 and built their stone house near this creek. Originally from Scotland, Charles came to California from Kansas in 1849.

Upstream from their home is a canyon and eighty-foot waterfall purchased by the late David Bouverie in 1947. Speaking of the area, now part of Bouverie Preserve, Bouverie said, "I bought the canyon and the waterfall from the surviving brother of prospector Walter Meddock. Living with Meddock was a sweet and badly treated woman who was paroled to him from what is now called the State Hospital. I have seen him send her out at the point of a gun to trap, catch and shoot what they ate. She dynamited the pools to get steelhead from the creek, but he preferred the jackrabbits and birds which she trapped and cooked for him. I saw an outhouse on which 20 or 30 skunk skins were stretched on boards. They ate the skunks and sold the skins." **B-2**

(see also Glen Ellen)

SUGARLOAF RIDGE STATE PARK's hills reminded early Kenwood residents of the large, conical shaped "sugar loaves" from which grocers in those days broke off pieces to sell by the pound. What is now the state park once served as ranch land for homesteaders and provided hardwood trees for charcoal (the trees ran out in 1893, though they have since come back.) Later, the land was used as a camp for Sonoma State Hospital and also leased for cattle grazing and hunting clubs. The land became a state park in 1964. **B-1**

(see also Embarcadero & Guilicos)

TEMELEC, the housing development off Arnold Drive, takes its name from a Miwok village that survived right up into pioneer times, after the American conquest of California. *Temelec's* meaning (sometimes spelled *temblec*) has not survived. Possibly the word has some connection to the verb root *tem-*, "to doctor." Natives from this area were known as Timbeleekees.

Bear Flagger Granville Swift, who made his fortune in mining and cattle, settled the Temelec area in 1851. In 1858 he began work on Temelec Hall, his southern-style mansion, using Indian slaves. Swift forced his workers to labor with cannonballs tied to their ankles and at night chained them to the walls in the basement of the mansion. (Indian slavery was legal in California until 1867, two years *after* slavery ended in the south.) *B-4*

(see also Sears Point)

THE LAKE THAT DISAPPEARED

TOLAY CREEK used to flow from a large body of water called Tolay Lake. Father Jose Altimira described the lake as being two-thirds of a mile long and varying from 400 feet to two-thirds of a mile wide. Although he said it was "named for a chief of the Indians who formerly populated this vicinity," this seems unlikely as there are no authentic examples of Miwoks naming places after people. In Lake Miwok, *tolay* (spelled *toleh* by linguists) means "wildcat", and a closely related verb means "to cock the ears". One source records the name of this lake as *Tolowa*, a word whose closest equivalent in Bodega Miwok is *toloma*, which also means "wildcat." Coincidentally or not, the high point on a nearby ridge is called Wildcat Mountain. German traveler Edward Vischer gives this description of the village of Tolay, on the shore of the lake, in October 1842:

"The *rancheria* [village] consisted of about fifteen or twenty cone-shaped huts of straw. There was only one opening through which one could crawl. Unless they were on duty with their white neighbors or on a fishing or hunting trip, old and young, male and female, lay inside around a fire. Knowledge of Spanish was of no use. . . we had to resort to signs and gestures if we wanted a drink of water from their basket-work pitcher. Similar vessels were used for cooking utensils. They do not place them over a fire, for fear that the close basket work may start to burn. Instead, they place heated rocks in them and make the contents boil.

The occupants of these huts show neither shyness nor readiness to oblige. Black and red tatoo-like stripes painted on their cheeks and chins and pitch-black hair falling loosely over their shoulders lend, particularly to the women, a strange appearance . . ."

continued

Vallejo mentions anchoring at *Punta Tulai* (Midshipman Point), probably his spelling of Tolay. About fifteen years after Vischer's visit, Lake Tolay was drained by William Bihler so he could plant potatoes. As the water went down, thousands of charmstones were revealed lying on the lake bottom. These special stones were believed to possess spiritual power and used as hunting amulets to attract game. On the hills surrounding the former lake are a number of baby rocks–large boulders with carved circles in them. A woman who wanted to get pregnant would sit on these rocks for fertility. *B-6*

TREADMILL ROAD is in Jack London State Park. During the 1800s most of the timber on Sonoma Mountain was cut for lumber and shipped to San Francisco. Along this road a donkey walked a treadmill to provide power for a buzz saw. ***Not on map***

TRINITY ROAD: When Jim Frazier, a dentist and theologian from Berkeley settled in the area with his religious followers, they applied for the establishment of a post office, to be called Trinity. The Postal Service denied their request because California already had a Trinity Post Office, so Frazier changed the spelling to Triniti, which was accepted in 1907. Frazier and his devotees spoke a dialect they called the Trinity language. The word "Trinity" referred to "a spiritual concept of peace." The community of Trinity was destroyed by fire in September 1923 and never rebuilt. The post office operated until 1935. Road signs installed in the 1950s changed the final "i" back to "y." *B-2*

TUBBS ISLAND was named for early landowner and cattle rancher Hiram Tubbs. *C-6*
(see also Skaggs Island)

TULI was the name of a village along Carriger Creek. Possibly there is a connection with the Miwok verb root *tul-*, meaning "to share" or "to whirl." (At least two tornados have occurred in this part of the valley since 1928) *B-4*
(see also Watmaugh Road)

TURTLE CREEK, really a stretch of Sonoma Creek in Kenwood, was named by the Green family, who moved there in 1946. There was also a Turtle Rock, where turtles congregated to sun themselves. The rock washed downstream one winter. These once-plentiful reptiles are now rarely spotted in the area, suggesting a recent change in the environment. *A-2*

VALLEY OF THE MOON, see SONOMA

MOUNT VEEDER was named for Reverend Peter Veeder, whose career spanned both religion and science. He was minister of the Presbyterian Church in Napa around 1860, president of City College in San Francisco from 1861-1871 and later served as professor of physics and astronomy at the Imperial University in Tokyo, Japan. *C-2*

WARFIELD, a stop on the Southern Pacific Railroad, was named for settlers Dr. Warfield and his wife Kate, who lived nearby. After her husband died, Kate became one of three "lady winemakers" in the area in the 1880s, a very unusual occupation for women in those days. *B-2*
(see also Glen Ellen & Hood Mountain)

WATMAUGH ROAD is probably named after James Watmough, Navy purser (officer in charge of accounts) in the Bay Area in the fall of 1846. He may have received a land grant from General Vallejo in this region of the valley. For unknown reasons, the spelling of the name was changed. *B-5*

THE SCHOOL THAT COULDN'T SIT STILL

Watmaugh School was established in 1857 as one of the first public schools in the valley. Constructed of wood, its one room housed students from first to eighth grade. There was a pump for water in the front yard and an outhouse in back.

Like an antsy student, the little schoolhouse had a hard time staying in one place: First established in a grove of oaks on what is now Leveroni Ranch, the school later moved a mile to the Champlin Ranch, and then to a site donated by Col. Rodgers. There it stayed until one spring day in 1928. Class was in session when the wind began building to a tremendous force. Looking out the window, two of the older boys saw a telephone pole bending in the wind. A freak cyclone was about to hit the school!

Jumping from their seats, the boys grabbed hold of the door frame and yelled to the other students to make two lines, holding tight to the child in front of them. When the cyclone hit, it picked up the schoolhouse, gave it a quarter turn and set it down again. Thanks to the boys' quick thinking, no one was injured. Forcing the door open, the children found shingles and other debris still flying around in the air. They took shelter on the porch until rides were arranged to take them home.

Originally, Watmaugh School had faced north and south; after the cyclone hit, it was oriented east and west. The building was left in its new position and continued to serve as a school for another twenty years before closing in 1947. In March 1983, another tornado hit El Verano, two miles north of the old Watmaugh School. *B-5*

(see also Tuli)

WHITNEY FALLS, at the head of Carriger Creek, is named after an early landowner who lost the property in a poker game. *A-3*

WILDCAT MOUNTAIN may have gotten its name from a bobcat that was seen or killed there. Or there may be some connection with the area's Miwok name. *C-6*
(see Tolay Creek for more on the Miwok connection)

WILDWATER was Jack London's name for Graham Creek, which bordered his ranch (now Jack London State Park). The name appears in his novel *Valley of the Moon* and still fits this pristine tributary of Sonoma Creek:

"They came to the rim of a deep canyon that seemed to penetrate to the heart of Sonoma Mountain. Billy stopped the wagon. The canyon was wildly beautiful. Tall redwoods lined its entire length . . .

They dropped down into the canyon, the road following a stream that sang under maples and alders. The sunset fires, refracted from the cloud-driftage of the autumn sky, bathed the canyon with crimson, in which ruddy-limbed madroños and wine-wooded manzanitas burned and smoldered. The air was aromatic with laurel. Wild grape-vines bridged the stream from tree to tree. Oaks of many sorts were veiled in lacy Spanish moss. Ferns and brakes grew lush beside the stream." *B-2*

from *Valley of the Moon,* by Jack London

WINGO, a tiny hamlet at the south end of the valley, may have been named by local duck and goose hunters for the wings of their prey, which were especially abundant in the area. Another story is that the name evolved from "where the wind goes" to "wind go" to "Wingo." This is an apt description for this place, where it seems the wind is always blowing. Nearby Pulpula, Father Altimira's first choice of a mission site, was abandoned for this reason. Travelers between

Sonoma and San Francisco in the late 19th century rode the train to Wingo, then transferred to a ferryboat for the trip across the bay.

Wingo was built by Chinese laborers, who piled up fill in the marsh one wheelbarrow at a time. Many employers preferred the Chinese because they would work eleven hours a day for a dollar in pay and provide their own food and shelter. Resentment by other workers, who felt the Chinese were taking away their jobs, resulted in much discrimination. Chinese were not allowed to become citizens or own land. In 1909, a bill was even passed by the California legislature to keep Asian children out of public schools. *C-5*
(see also China Slough, Chinatown, Norfolk & Poppe's Landing)

WOLF HOUSE, Jack London's dream mansion, was just weeks from completion when it burned down in 1913. Arson was suspected; fire experts now believe spontaneous combustion of oily rags was the cause. Wolves feature prominently in a number of London's tales. *The Son of the Wolf* was his first published book, and *The Call of the Wild* his first big success. If the following story is true, perhaps London's spirit is still here, in wolf-form. *A-3*
(see also Jack London State Park)

THE GHOST DOG OF GLEN ELLEN

One warm day in 1996, a Glen Ellen shopkeeper had the door of her business propped open. Looking up from behind the counter, she was surprised to find a large, white, wolf-like dog with unusual yellow eyes sitting in the middle of her store. Since the animal appeared friendly, she patted it on the head and, thinking it might be thirsty, went to fill a bowl with water. On the way back, she saw the dog walking out the door and turning to the right. Only a few steps behind, she followed after, hoping to coax it back for a drink. When she got outside, the dog was nowhere to be seen. Because the front of her building is quite long, it seemed impossible the animal could have slipped around a corner so fast. The dog had apparently just disappeared into thin air!

A dog matching this description has been seen by several other Glen Ellen residents, who say it never lets them approach too closely. As far as we know, the shopkeeper is the only person who has actually touched this mysterious animal.

WUKILIWA was a Miwok village near Agua Caliente, and also probably the name of the hot springs which are abundant in the area. Combining *wuki,* meaning "fire" or "hot," and *liwa,* the word for water, it means "Hot Water". *B-3*
(see also Agua Caliente & Boyes Hot Springs)

YULUPA is a Miwok name appearing in several places. There's a Yulupa Spring on the former Carriger Ranch west of El Verano. Yulupa Creek feeds into Sonoma Creek between Kenwood and Glen Ellen, and mission records list a village called *Yulupa* in that area. Local lore also says *Yulupa* was the Miwok name for Bennett Mountain. *A-2*
(see story below)

WHO REALLY NAMED THE GOLDEN GATE

Strangely enough, *yulupa* is said to have been the original name for both Bennett Mountain and San Francisco's Golden Gate. Unraveling the mystery of why two such different places would share the same name requires delving into Miwok language as well as some speculation.

Yulupa is an interesting word that may have no exact English translation. Its meaning centers around things that are bright and shiny, like crystals, water and sunsets. For people living in many parts of Sonoma Valley, the sun goes down near Bennett Mountain for much of the year, putting bright colors in the sky there, thus it was called *yulupa*. Now imagine living on the northern shore of San Francisco Bay, as some Miwoks did, looking out through the Golden Gate. On late afternoons, when the sun was low and reflecting off the Pacific, you would see a glare shining through the Golden Gate-perhaps another form of *yulupa*. And an hour or two later the bright colors of the sunset would appear in the same area, just as they do near Bennett Mountain.

In Spanish and Mexican times, the Gate was known as "Sunset Strait." John C. Fremont said the name *Chrysopylae*, "Golden Gate" in Greek, came to him as he watched the sunset change the waters of the harbor entrance to gold. Indeed, "golden" may be one of the closest English equivalents to *yulupa* and Fremont's claim to authorship notwithstanding, the concept of "Golden Gate" may date back thousands of years.

(see also Bennett Mountain, Carriger Creek & Mountain of the Burning Bird)

Yulupa
(Bennett Mountain)
as seen from Glen Ellen

PLACE NAMES OF SPECIAL INTEREST

NATIVE AMERICAN
(before 1823)

Chiucuyem
Guilicos
Hu'tci
Lac
Mayacamas
Mtn. of the Burning Bird
  (possible translation)
Oona-pa'is
Petaluma
Pulpula
Sonoma
Temelec
Tolay Creek
Tuli
Wukiliwa
Yulupa

SPANISH/MEXICAN ERA
(circa 1810 - 1846)

Adobe Canyon
Agua Caliente
Calabazas Creek
Carneros
Embarcadero
Mission San Francisco Solano
New San Francisco

AMERICAN
PIONEER ERA
(1846 to 1875)

Asbury Creek
Bear Creek
Bennett Mountain
Bihler Slough
Carriger Creek
Champlin Creek
Cooper's Bridge
Fowler Creek
Glen Ellen
Haraszthy Creek
Hoeppner's Branch
Hood Mountain
Hooker Creek
Hudson's Corner
Kohler Creek
Locust Grove
Mammy Pleasant's Cave
Nathanson Creek
Nunns Canyon
San Luis
Schellville
Schocken Hill
Secret Pasture
Sears Point
Stuart Creek
Watmaugh Road

TURN
OF THE CENTURY
(1875 to 1925)

Annadel State Park
Boyes Hot Springs
Chinatown
El Verano
Kenwood
Jack London State Park
Lewis Creek
Treadmill Road
Trinity Road
Wildwater
Wingo
Wolf House

SINCE 1930

Arnold Drive
Hippie Hollow
Qaleqoci Creek
Skaggs Island
Sky Rock
Turtle Creek

WINEMAKING

Glen Ellen
Haraszthy Creek
Kohler Creek
Madrone Road
Pansy Valley

TRANSPORTATION

Annadel State Park
El Verano
Embarcadero
Kenwood
Norfolk
Poppe's Landing
Schellville
Schocken Hill

Skaggs Island
Steamboat Slough
Stage Gulch Road
Stofen's Landing
Wingo

Author's Comments:
Deciphering the Language of the Land

Researching the origins and meanings of Sonoma Valley place names required many hours of detective work, looking through old books and documents searching for clues, following hunches, and making educated guesses. Like a geologist, I had to dig through many layers of history. Some place names are as tough as diamonds, holding their own as cultures and languages shift around them. Others are soft as sandstone, quickly eroded and soon forgotten. A few are even metamorphic, changing over time as they are adopted by succeeding waves of immigrants.

As you might expect, Native American names were the trickiest to decipher. Before European contact, more than 100 languages were spoken in California, and most of these had several dialects. People speaking different languages often lived just over the hill or along neighboring creeks and many early Californians were fluent in several languages. Two hundred years ago you would have found speakers of Coast Miwok, Wappo and Wintun (sometimes called Patwin) all living within a dozen miles of present-day Sonoma Plaza. For place names from this era, I had to rely on early written accounts of Sonoma Valley, which are themselves in several languages. Speakers of English and Spanish, hearing the same word, usually spelled it differently. For example, a village near Kenwood was spelled Guilucos by the Mexicans and Wilikos by the Americans. This makes sense if you know that a Spanish "g" is sometimes pronounced like an English "w".

By looking at various spellings and pronouncing them in the language in which they were written, I was able to get a feel for the word's original sound. Next I checked to see if a similar-sounding word existed in any of the native languages of Sonoma Valley. I consulted Bodega and Lake Miwok (dialects of Coast Miwok) dictionaries, a Wappo dictionary, and a Tcho-ko-yem (also spelled Chiucuyem) vocabulary of about 150 words collected in 1851 from survivors of this Sonoma Miwok tribelet. I was unable to locate a Wintun dictionary. I also studied Miwok and Wappo place names with known meanings outside Sonoma Valley, to get a feel for their flavor and style.

Where I found words that closely matched local place names, I compared their meaning to what exists (or existed) at each particular site. For example, *Pulpula*, a village in the southern part of the valley, sounds very close to *polpol*, a Lake Miwok word meaning "pond". As a matter of fact the founder of Sonoma's

Mission, Father Jose Altimira, mentioned a number of ponds in the area in his 1823 journal, and they're still there today. The convergence of these two pieces of evidence makes a strong case for the original meaning of *Pulpula* being "ponds".

One pitfall I've tried to avoid is the tendency of outsiders to romanticize Native American cultures. For this reason, General Vallejo's translations probably shouldn't be taken at face value. Though he had some knowledge of Suisun, the Wintun language spoken by his friend Chief Solano, most of Vallejo's interpretations appear to be inaccurate. A good example is *Petaluma*, a village name which he took for his huge rancho, saying it meant "Oh Fair Vale!", a phrase full of Victorian romanticism. Tom Smith, a Miwok elder interviewed in the 1930s, said "*petaluma* means "back" in my language." Anthropologist Samuel Barrett, who studied Coast Miwok culture at the turn of the 20th century, said *petaluma* is a composite of *pe'ta* meaning flat, and *luma* meaning back. He gave the whole meaning as "slope-back", a good description of the hills in this area west of Sonoma Valley, especially Sonoma Mountain as seen from modern-day Petaluma. A Lake Miwok dictionary compiled by linguist Catherine Callaghan in 1965 lists *luuma* as the word for "back".

Vallejo's misinterpretations are not suprising. In his era, no one realized how linguistically complex California was. American Richard Henry Dana, who chronicled a visit to California in 1835 in *Two Years Before the Mast*, thought all the natives from San Diego to San Francisco spoke the same language. Indigenous culture and language were considered primitive and almost unworthy of notice. Along with this prejudice was the fact that the Sonoma Mission had gathered neophytes from an area that stretched from the coast to the Sacramento River. At least six languages were probably being spoken at the Sonoma Mission when Vallejo arrived in 1834, so it's no surprise that he was confused about the language of Sonoma's original inhabitants. The General probably had no way of knowing that using Suisun to translate Miwok names was like interpreting German with an Italian dictionary! But perhaps we should forgive the General if his creativity often exceeded his accuracy when it came to native languages. It was probably another of his misinterpretations that gave us one of our most poetic local place names, "Valley of the Moon."

There must have been hundreds of places already named when the first Mexican missionaries and soldiers settled Sonoma Valley in the early 19th century. Since the Mexicans sometimes named places after people (mostly saints), they assumed the native people did too. Father Altimira said Tolay Lake was "named for the chief of the Indians." In fact, there are no authenticated instances of Coast Miwoks naming places after people, though they did name *people after places*. A number of Miwok place names were adopted by the Mexican pioneers, who often hispanicized the names. For example, Rancho Huichica probably got its name from *hu'tci*, a former village near the present-day Sonoma Plaza. Another word bearing the imprint of successive waves of immigrants is Los Guilicos. It appears that this began as the tribal name *guiluc*, altered in Spanish to *Guilucos*, then altered and mispelled by an American surveyor to Los Guilicos. At least one name has changed languages without changing meaning: a place called *wukiliwa* ("hot water") by the Miwoks, became *Agua Caliente* ("hot water") in Mexican times. English names for this part of the valley include Boyes Hot Springs, Fetters Hot Springs or just "the Springs."

Surprisingly few Spanish names survived the coming of the American era, which began with the Bear Flag Rebellion in 1846. English quickly became Sonoma Valley's dominant language. It is very common in English to name places after people, and soon names like Schellville, Glen Ellen and Mount Veeder had taken up residence on the land. While some places are named with the deliberate intention of commemorating some individual, I believe much of the naming which took place in Sonoma in the mid-19th century was a less formal and more neighborly affair. Solomon Schocken owned the hill where many men labored making cobblestones, so it became known as Schocken Hill. The Nathansons lived along a creek north of town, so everyone called it Nathanson Creek. Indeed, it would probably be most accurate to think of a number of local places as being named after families rather than individuals.

Each layer of history has added names to Sonoma Valley. A handful have survived for perhaps thousands of years, as cultures and languages shifted around them. Who knows how many have come and gone and been forgotten? Most of the names remembered in this book, as well as the ones in common use, had their origins in the second half of the nineteenth century. In the twentieth century the naming process has slowed to a crawl, but has never completely stopped. Just last year Qaleqoci Creek got its name, and Sky Rock and Hippie Hollow are also relative newcomers on the map. Time moves on, new names appear and old ones melt away. In some distant future, this place will have a different name.

Published Sources

Alexander, James B. *Sonoma Valley Legacy.*

Altimira, Jose. *Diario de la expedicion verificada con objecto de reconocer terrenos para la nueva planta de las Mision de Nuestro Padre San Francisco principiada le dia 25 de Junio de 1823* [Bancroft Library collection].

Baker, Sue & Forrest, Audrey B. *Secrets of El Verano In the Valley of the Moon.*

Calkin, Victoria. *The Wappo People.*

Callaghan, Catherine. *Lake Miwok Dictionary.*

Catherine, Callaghan. *Bodega Miwok Dictionary.*

Collier, Mary & Thalman, Sylvia [Editors]. *Interviews with Tom Smith & Maria Copa; Isabel Kelly's Notes on the Coast Miwok Indians of Marin and Southern Sonoma Counties, California.*

Eliade, Mircea. *The Encyclopedia of Religion.*

Finley, Latimer. *History of Sonoma County.*

Glotzbach, Bob. *Childhood Memories of Glen Ellen.*

Gudde, Erwin. *California Place Names.*

Hansen, Harvey J. & Miller, Jeanne Thurlow. *Wild Oats in Eden, Sonoma County in the 19th Century.*

Heizer, Robert. *The Natural World of the California Indians.*

Illustrated Atlas of Sonoma County, 1897.

Latta, Frank F. *Joaquin Murrieta and his Horse Gangs.*

LeBaron, Gaye, Blackman, Dee & others. *Santa Rosa, A Nineteenth Century Town.*

Lee, Hector, Heroes. *Villains & Ghosts; Folklore of Old California.*

Marryat, Frank. *North Bay Journal and Visits to Gold Rush San Francisco.*

McKittrick, Myrtle M. *Vallejo, Son of California.*

Miwok Archeological Preserve of Marin. *Dawn of the World; Stories told by Coast Miwok Indians.*

Morgan, Dale. *Overland in 1846; Diaries and Letters of the California-Oregon Trail.*

Murphy, Celeste. *The People of the Pueblo, The Story of Sonoma.*

O'Callaghan, Trissa. *Our Mission's Saint, Francisco Solano.* Sonoma Index-Tribune. May 24, 1973.

Parmelee, Robert D. *Pioneer Sonoma.*

Sand, Dallyce. *Kenwood, Yesterday and Today.*

Smilie, Robert S. *The Sonoma Mission.*

Sonoma Index-Tribune. *Centennial Edition. July, 1979.*

Sonoma Valley Historical Society. *Saga of Sonoma in the Valley of the Moon.*

Thompson, Robert. *Sonoma County Atlas. 1877.*

Other Sources

Individuals and organizations who contributed stories and information for this book include:

Susheel Bibbs
Bouverie Preserve
Marion Britton
Susan Bundschu
Jabez W. Churchill
Sylvia Crawford
Bob Glotzbach

Liz Parsons
Dallyce Sand
Milo Shepard
Pat & Win Smith
Sonoma Valley Historical Society
Vasquez House
Margaret Wiltshire

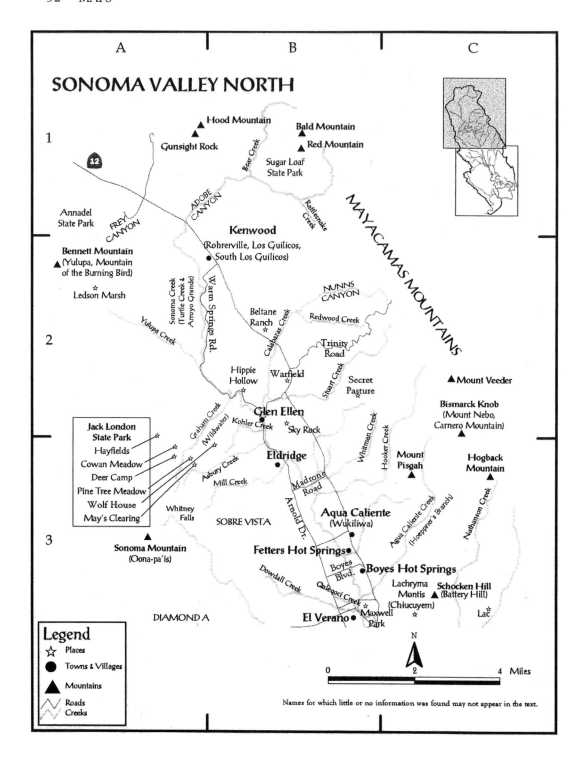

SONOMA VALLEY NORTH

A   B   C

12

1

▲ Hood Mountain

Gunsight Rock ▲

▲ Bald Mountain

▲ Red Mountain

Bear Creek

Sugar Loaf
State Park

ADOBE CANYON

Rattlesnake Creek

MAYACAMAS MOUNTAINS

Annadel
State Park

FREY CANYON

Kenwood
(Rohrerville, Los Guilicos,
● South Los Guilicos)

Bennett Mountain
▲ (Yulupa, Mountain
of the Burning Bird)

☆ Ledson Marsh

Sonoma Creek
(Turtle Creek &
Arroyo Grande)

Warm Springs Rd.

NUNNS
CANYON

Yulupa Creek

Beltane
Ranch

Calabazas Creek

Redwood Creek

Trinity
Road

Shatt Creek

2

Hippie
Hollow
☆

Warfield
☆

Secret
Pasture

▲ Mount Veeder

Bismarck Knob
(Mount Nebo,
Carnero Mountain)
▲

Jack London
State Park ☆
Hayfields ☆
Cowan Meadow ☆
Deer Camp
Pine Tree Meadow
Wolf House
May's Clearing

Graham Creek

Wildwater

Kohler Creek

Glen Ellen
●

☆ Sky Rock

Whitman Creek

Hooker Creek

Mount
Pisgah
▲

Hogback
Mountain
▲

Asbury Creek

Eldridge
●

Mill Creek

Madrone Road

Whitney
Falls

SOBRE VISTA

Arnold Dr.

Aqua Caliente
(Wukiliwa)
●

Agua Caliente Creek
(Hoepner's Branch)

Nathanson Creek

3

Sonoma Mountain
▲ (Oona-pa´is)

Fetters Hot Springs ●

Boyes
Blvd.

● **Boyes Hot Springs**

Dowdall Creek

Qalegoci Creek

Lachryma
Montis
(Chiucuyem)
☆

Schocken Hill
▲ (Battery Hill)

Lac ☆

DIAMOND A

El Verano ●

● Maxwell
Park

Legend
☆   Places
●   Towns & Villages
▲   Mountains
〜   Roads
    Creeks

N

0   2   4   Miles

Names for which little or no information was found may not appear in the text.

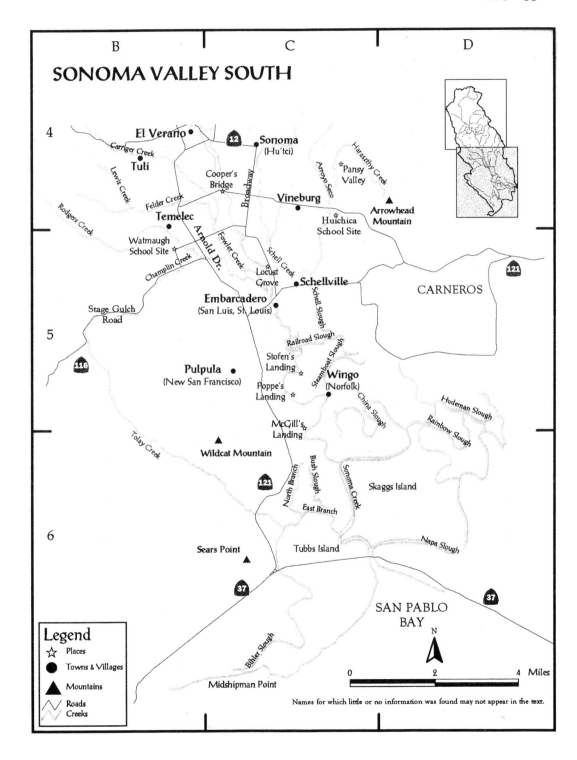

SONOMA VALLEY SOUTH

B   C   D

4

El Verano
Carriger Creek
12
Sonoma
(Hu'tci)
Tuli
Harasthy Creek
Lewis Creek
Cooper's
Bridge
Broadway
Pansy
Valley
Arroyo Seco
Felder Creek
Vineburg
Rodgers Creek
Temelec
Huichica
School Site
Arrowhead
Mountain
Watmaugh
School Site
Arnold Dr.
Fowler Creek
Champlin Creek
Schell Creek
Locust
Grove
Schellville
CARNEROS
121
Embarcadero
(San Luis, St. Louis)
Schell Slough

5

Stage Gulch
Road
Railroad Slough
Steamboat Slough
116
Pulpula
(New San Francisco)
Stofen's
Landing
Wingo
(Norfolk)
Poppe's
Landing
China Slough
Hudeman Slough
Rainbow Slough
McGill's
Landing
Tolay Creek
Wildcat Mountain
121
North Branch
Bush Slough
Sonoma Creek
Skaggs Island
East Branch

6

Sears Point
Tubbs Island
Napa Slough
37
SAN PABLO
BAY
N

Legend
☆ Places
● Towns & Villages
▲ Mountains
⋀ Roads
⁄⁄ Creeks

Bihler Slough
Midshipman Point

37

0   2   4   Miles

Names for which little or no information was found may not appear in the text.

ABOUT THE AUTHOR

Freelance writer and poet Arthur Dawson lives in Glen Ellen with his wife Jill and baby daughter Kyrie. His work has appeared in *Outside* magazine, *Travelers' Tales Guides*, the *Kenwood Press* and numerous poetry magazines. He has taught with California Poets In the Schools for many years, inspiring students of all ages. Recently he developed and directed *A Song of Place*, a program of poetry workshops focusing on the cultural and natural history of Sonoma Valley. A volume of poems from this project will be available in late 1998.

Before coming to Sonoma Valley in 1989, Arthur and Jill spent three years traveling around the world, journeying by sailboat, elephant, dugout canoe, steam train, and at least one bus with no brakes. His book about that trip, *A Passport From the Elements*, is currently on its own journey in search of a publisher. *The Stories Behind Sonoma Valley Place Names* is his second book.

Someday he'd like to see snow in Glen Ellen, some steelhead in Asbury Creek, and a tornado in El Verano (hopefully harmless). One of these days he's going to paddle a kayak from Sonoma's Embarcadero to Midshipman Point.